Books of Merit

A Quiet Courage

A Quiet Courage

Inspiring Stories from All of Us

Paula Todd

Thomas Allen Publishers
Toronto

National Library of Canada Cataloguing in Publication

Todd, Paula, 1959–
A quiet courage : inspiring stories from all of us / Paula Todd.

ISBN 0-88762-155-4

1. Canada—Biography.   2. Courage—Anecdotes.   I. Title.

FC25.T63 2004   971'.009'9   C2004-902573-2

Editor: Patrick Crean
Jacket design: Bill Douglas @ The Bang
Jacket image: Johner / Photonica

Photo credits: courtesy Homewood Corporation (Cunningham); Max Brown (Brown); Dr. Donald Payne (Abai); Gia Lucchetta (Dane); courtesy Rose Handy (Handy); Lisa Scale (Savoia); Brenda Brizeula (Castrillon); Taralea Cutler (Ribreau); Shawn McDonald (Anderson); Don Lindsay (Lindsay); Richard Seck (Alam); courtesy Kent Laidlaw (Laidlaw)

Published by Thomas Allen Publishers,
a division of Thomas Allen & Son Limited,
145 Front Street East, Suite 209,
Toronto, Ontario M5A 1E3 Canada

www.thomas-allen.com

ONTARIO ARTS COUNCIL
CONSEIL DES ARTS DE L'ONTARIO

Canada Council
for the Arts

The publisher gratefully acknowledges the support of
the Ontario Arts Council for its publishing program.

We acknowledge the support of the Canada Council for the Arts, which
last year invested $21.7 million in writing and publishing throughout Canada.

We acknowledge the Government of Ontario through the
Ontario Media Development Corporation's Ontario Book Initiative.

We acknowledge the financial support of the Government of Canada through the
Book Publishing Industry Development Program (BPIDP) for our publishing activities.

09 08 07 06 05   3 4 5 6 7

Printed and bound in Canada

For Doug

Contents

Preface

The Irish author Edna O'Brien once wondered about the formula for survival. "Looking back I realize that I am one of the luckiest people in the world, since no matter how down I go something brings me back. Is it God's grace or just peasant resilience?"

I have discovered that there are as many answers to that question as there are people asking it.

This is a book about men and women who survived some of the worst life has to offer, returned from the brink, rose above and went beyond the darkness in life.

They are people who allowed me into their lives and their hearts, and shared their deepest hurt. They have lived all over the world, done every type of work, known great wealth and poverty, too. But all of them share the conviction that coming through chaos has made them see more clearly, value life more deeply and discover in themselves strengths that might otherwise have gone untapped.

And I found them not by looking for tragedy, but while tracking down success. A few years ago, we wanted to create a different type of television interview program at TVOntario, the largest educational broadcaster in Canada. We wanted to dig beneath the biographical details of achievers and into their psyches to discover what made them tick. We weren't interested in the overexposed exploits of celebrities, who are too often applauded—and denigrated—for doing nothing very special at all.

Instead, we wanted to explore the lives of people who—with no acclaim, no fanfare and no spotlights—simply did exceptional things.

As interview subjects, we selected men and women who stood out in their communities or professional fields—an outspoken educator, a heroic policewoman, a respected physician—and tried to analyze the source of the strength of character that others so admired. I was eager to learn their secrets; what were the keys to their success—a great education, a perfect marriage, a nurturing childhood?

And that's when I got a shock.

The truth was that they had few or none of those advantages. In fact, many of these superstars came from the worst backgrounds imaginable. With remarkable consistency, the men and women I questioned about success talked about failure. Or loss. Or huge obstacles. All of them could point to a tragedy, a pivotal, character-defining event or phase in their life from which—after great struggle—they emerged stronger and more passionate about living.

I discovered that the difference between a routine life and a robust one was not necessarily privilege, birthright, education or a harmonious home. The difference could also be loss, illness, disability, crime, addiction or abuse. More specifically, it was the journey taken in overcoming the adversity, and the skills honed in doing so, that transformed the average individual into an exceptional one.

From the many successful people I interviewed over several years there emerged a study in survival; and something more for which I wish there was a word—*thrival*. Because when human beings are able to transcend suffering, failure and calamity, it seems that the process can free up vast potential: against astounding odds they fight to go forward, unwilling to be crushed, and some of them go beyond *surviving* to *thriving*.

Incredibly, some thrivers have told me they cannot wholeheartedly regret what happened to them—the crippling accident, a painful loss, a serious illness, a grave error—because they believe that without it they would not be the much more accomplished, emotionally attuned person they are today. Without that which hurt them, derailed them, almost destroyed them, they believe they might never have undergone the forced emotional evolution that gave birth to their new, stronger self.

I have seen proof that the worst events of our lives need not crush us, but can elevate us. That loss, injustice and setbacks need not diminish us, but can ultimately shore us up, make us bigger and stronger. That tragedy, while unwelcome, can also contribute to our worth and enhance our life as much as, if not more than, a promotion or a victory.

It occurs to me, too, that many of us may be undermining our relationships and our public institutions—including politics—by preferring people with "a clean slate" over those who've survived upset and tragedy. It is the survivor who may often be better equipped than the neophyte to love and to lead.

Courage is not always immediate, not always bold: it flutters to life in the torture chambers of Ethiopia; it rallies in cancer clinics; it finds its true voice in a dark alley after turning a hundred tricks. You will not necessarily like everyone you meet on these pages, but I guarantee that you will want to borrow some of their life-saving tools.

Almost immediately after TVOntario's *Person 2 Person with Paula Todd* went on the air, we were swamped with letters. Viewers said they were astonished and humbled by the courage of the people we profiled. They said they had renewed faith in the strength of the human spirit. Many told us they watched the interviews again and again in repeats, or taped the programs so they could view them when they needed inspiration in their own lives.

But more than anything, viewers asked for more—for fuller descriptions of what these extraordinary people had overcome, more insights into their secrets of survival. And they wanted it in the form of a book they could keep by their bed or at their office, a book they could give to others who were facing life's inevitable challenges.

And so I went back to some of the people who had already given so much to the camera and asked them to give more for the page. We talked, we wrote to each other and, for a while, I retraced the paths of the courageous. Some days and some nights the experience was harrowing—reliving a man's near-death on a skidding motorcycle; witnessing the cost of alcoholism; imagining the blood of friends trickling away in a torture chamber. There were times when I had to lie on the floor and wait for new strength to write. I cannot imagine living much of what I will tell you about here. But I know that these are among the most magnificent people I will ever meet and I want you to know them, too.

Also extraordinary is their generosity in sharing these private tales. As Mary Brown, the young mother diagnosed with colon cancer and given six months to live, explains: "When you talk about it, when you share your own story, no one else can hurt you with it."

Dr. Graeme Cunningham, a former president of Ontario's College of Physicians and Surgeons, who spent many years of his life as a closet alcoholic says, "I put it out there. I tell my story so I can keep it." It is only shame that lives in silence.

As Doug Dane, the loving father and articulate business whiz who was reared by violent alcoholics and abused by pedophiles assures us, "So many of us have experienced so many hard times. The more you talk, the more you realize how many people are like you, and the shame falls away."

This book is for all the people who asked me to find out more about courage and for all the people who helped me do so.

Finding Courage
Where You Least Expect It

I am often asked to name the most interesting person I've ever interviewed, or the most fascinating story I've covered. But the question is impossible to answer. After more than twenty years as a journalist, I have heard too many extraordinary tales, met too many fascinating people, to choose just one.

Ask me, though, to name the most disappointing, the most disillusioning interview I've ever conducted. That one is easy: Elisabeth Kübler-Ross, March 2002, Phoenix, Arizona.

I want to tell you about that one because the most dismal interview I ever had turned out to be in many ways the most inspiring. It changed my way of seeing the world.

Kübler-Ross is the internationally renowned psychiatrist who identified the five stages of grief: denial, anger, bargaining, depression and acceptance. She has more than twenty honorary degrees. Her many books and essays have been translated into dozens of languages, and she has spent much of her own life helping other people die. Her best-selling treatise, *On Death and Dying* (1969), revolutionized the way the Western world confronts death.

But it was a much more recent book that attracted me. *Life Lessons*, published in 2000 by Kübler-Ross and David Kessler, instructs us to use the lessons recognized as we are dying to enhance the quality of whatever life remains. Kübler-Ross, who built a career recording deathbed confessions, laments the fact that people wait until the last moments of their lives to realize they should have been kinder, wiser, more loving; they should have taken more risks, been more careful, controlled their anger, expressed their anger, or believed more in the power of the universe.

"Our lessons in life involve working on our smallness, getting rid of our negativity and finding the best in ourselves and each other," she writes. Living closer to the bone, nearer to our own authentic self, she says, will also allow us to die more peacefully.

These observations made a strong impression on me. For several years I'd been hosting a television program in Canada, interviewing remarkable but relatively unknown people from around the world. I was startled to discover the number of successful, fulfilled individuals who'd lived through hell. I became consumed with figuring out where these survivors dug for the extra strength that allowed them to continue. How had they managed to learn their "life lessons" so early and use them to such advantage? I read, I researched, I interviewed. I wanted to learn their secrets.

I found Kübler-Ross's *Life Lessons* in one of my favourite places— an airport bookstore—and finished it on a flight from Toronto to Calgary. It was exciting. She surely understood a great deal about this psychological journey from adversity to enlightenment. Suddenly, I was desperate to interview *her* before it was too late.

But gaining an audience with the Swiss-born doctor turned out to be a very difficult task: she was retired, in her seventies, reclusive and living deep in the Arizona desert. She'd had a series of strokes and rarely granted interviews. But I *needed* to see her.

Persistence paid off, especially through the efforts of Karen Pinker, a Toronto producer who lined up the momentous interview. Thorough and principled, Pinker made sure Kübler-Ross knew when and why we were coming and how much this experience would mean to our program. Despite having already conducted thousands of interviews for print and television, I was excited.

Logistically, it was a big deal, too. We flew thousands of miles from Toronto to Phoenix, picked up a jeep and a crew and set out to find the oracle.

We bump up and down barren roads of orange dust, past claw-like trees and battered boulders. Finally, we locate her large adobe home, crammed with baskets and artwork, the souvenirs of a fascinating life and successful career.

What did I expect? Brilliance, insight, compassion? Well, yes. That's how she sounds in her book.

What did I find? Little of the above. And worse.

She is one of the angriest, most difficult people I have ever met.

At first, despite our careful arrangements and lengthy trip, she refuses to see us. We stand in the desert, panicking. Finally, one of her attendants emerges to say that the doctor has changed her mind and will speak—but only to me.

I close the door behind me. Kübler-Ross's home is dark and cool, the wide terra cotta tiles silky under my feet. To get to her, I have to walk through a large open kitchen, stocked as if for war with rations of canned and packaged goods piled on the counters, on the floor and bulging from cupboards.

Directly ahead of the kitchen on the right is a large living room draped in darkness. To the left is a smaller room, in which Kübler-Ross has set up camp. It is cramped and dingy. Her bed is pushed up against the far wall; beside it, within a few difficult steps, there's a big chair, layered with old blankets and sheets, and a coffee table piled with papers, dirty dishes and empty food containers. Ashtrays full of cigarette butts perch precariously on abandoned mail. She will light a cigarette and then forget it as it burns into a long snake of ash.

"What do you want? Go away," she snaps. Not the cordial reception I'm used to on the job; not the first impression I was hoping to make.

She is curled up on her bed, wrapped in a baggy blue hospital gown. Her side table is covered in dust. I come closer, tentatively, and explain we've arranged an interview to talk about her work.

"Life is shit. Go away," she growls, and turns her head. "Shit, shit, shit."

Her hostility frightens me. Her rage shocks me. No one warned me about this odd behaviour. No one mentioned that there was something pricklier than the cactus in this desert. And now I'm worried that we've come all this way and won't get the story, worried that the woman behind the positive philosophy so many have found uplifting may turn out to be a fiction, and on a personal level, afraid that my emerging commitment to understanding the sacred in life is about to implode.

Now, to be fair to Kübler-Ross, she'd suffered a series of strokes and was frustrated by the physical limits she now faced. There were likely psychological side effects as well. Clearly, she had forgotten or grown tired of traditional social conventions. Wanting to be released from her physical prison of disability, she grew more impatient and angry each day.

And it is clear, too, that she was aware of her behaviour. As she wrote in her 2000 book, *Life Lessons*, "So many people have told me how much they appreciate my stages on death and dying, of which anger is one. But now, so many people in my life disappeared when I became angry myself . . . It's as if they loved my stages but didn't like me being in one of them. But those who stayed with me allowed me to be, not judging me or my anger, and that helped to dissipate it."

But now—with those published words years behind her it is clear she is *still* in the grip of rage, that her anger is potent. And though her books tell the rest of us that we must work hard to learn our life lessons before we die, she seems to be resisting her own theory.

I try to stay calm and soothing. Perhaps, I think, she hasn't been properly prepared for our visit. I explain how much her work means to the world, and how valuable her insights would be for us, especially now that she is at the critical junction of life and death.

"It's all bullshit," she yells, and reaches out to hit my arm. "I give you a karate chop. Chop, chop, chop." Even now, after years of working in America and a long marriage to a New Yorker, she still has a thick German accent.

Breathe. Swallow. I ask, "Why do you want to hit me?"

"Life is bullshit. I hate it. I want to die. It's boring, boring, boring. Bullshit."

The idealist in me folds. I see this for what it is: I am in a dark room in the middle of the desert with an old woman who is pretending to hit me, while good people wait outside in the burning sun. I decide then that no matter how experienced she is, how fascinating her work, I have learned enough in life—including her very own "life lessons"—to know that I am not going to sit here for several hours while she uses me as an emotional and physical punching bag.

So, I follow her lead.

Look, I tell her, we've come a long way. I've read your books. A lot of people have gone to a great deal of trouble to be here. You have no reason for treating us this way. If you didn't want to see us, you should have said so long ago.

Besides, why does she write about life if all she wants to do is die?

At that I see a little laugh bloom in her eyes as she looks at me cagily. She *likes* this performance of hers: the crazy woman with the electrified hair, her nightgown pulled high on her thigh, railing at life, hitting out at it. It's as if I'm a laboratory rat being exposed to bizarre stimuli while she notes my responses. She's bored, all right, and she has nothing to play with but me.

"Okay," she says, "you can stay and talk to me, but no one else can come in here. Only you!"

Summoned into Kübler-Ross's inner sanctum, it seems I have passed some odd test. But it's too late: now I am as stubborn as she.

Impossible, I say.

Unreasonable, I say.

Chop! Chop! Chop!

I am here to film her—she and her son have known for a long time we were coming—and I cannot do that alone. The producer, camera crew and sound recordist must come in, too. I tell her they will be very respectful and that she will retain control, able to tell them to leave if they annoy her.

She laughs a little, a funny gravelly sound. She likes this. "Fine," she growls, but the ice is gone.

She insists we first seat her in the chair, then takes a swat at the sound recordist as he attaches her microphone. She chastises us, telling us to hurry up, flirting with the men in the crew—none of them older than thirty. She turns her head to and fro, seeming to know where the camera lingers. She likes the attention.

She does not, however, like all of my questions. She does not want to talk about her theories of death and dying—or life and living, for that matter—repeating often that she wants to die as soon as possible. She refuses to discuss any research that contradicts her own theories, and is inclined not to talk when I ask about allegations that she borrowed from her colleagues' work while writing her opus on death.

She will talk about her childhood, the horrid experience, she says, of being a triplet. And she wants to talk about the fifty "spirits" who now live in the house with her, the lingering souls of dead loved ones or strangers who keep her company. She believes deeply in the afterlife and behaves much of the time as if she's already there. Sometimes her sense of humour twinkles.

She confides that she thinks God is angry at her, punishing her by keeping her on earth when she lacks the mobility to enjoy anything, especially the outdoors and her garden. She admits she is struggling to learn her own life lessons—patience, for example—but feels more like fighting these days.

We play tug-of-war: me hoping she'll talk about the meaning of life, her trying to get me into the kitchen to cook for her. There's no question she's being cared for—visitors, fans, friends, hangers-on come and go, offering to run errands and do her bidding. But she is hungry *now*.

So, while the crew and producer wait tensely for the real interview to begin, she shouts instructions from her chair. New potatoes, boiled just so, firm but not mushy. I dress them with fresh pale butter and a little salt and pepper, careful to quarter them—as ordered—but keep intact the delicate brown skin. She tells me I must wait until she's eaten to speak to her again. But next she wants soup.

I make the soup while she shakes the remote control at the television, jumping from channel to snowy channel, the sound so loud it drowns out thought.

The mail carrier arrives with a bundle of envelopes and parcels, mainly fan letters and gifts from strangers. She doesn't bother looking. Now she's yelling again that she doesn't want the door open, that there are too many people in the room, that life is hell and she is mad at God.

"Is it always like this?" I ask the mail carrier while I stir Kübler-Ross's lunch. He grimaces politely. "Pretty much, but she's okay."

When Pinker and I finally face the fact that the interview, despite our efforts, isn't going to sustain the hour-long program we'd envisioned, Kübler-Ross nods and says she has something to ask before we leave her.

My heart skips. Am I finally going to receive one of those famous insights for which students and disciples make the long trek to her door?

"Yes?" I say.

"Make me a cheese tray before you go. A good one," she says.

So I do, musing about the mysteries of life as I root through the crammed refrigerator of one of the world's most famous psychiatrists, searching for a sufficient variety of cheeses to escape her criticism. I bring in the dish, neatly arranged.

"Hmm . . . good," she says. "Well, move me to the bed." The crew has fled, so I lift Kübler-Ross as gently as possible and struggle to help her into her wheelchair and then out again and up into her bed. I tuck her in. I thank her for her time and for her books.

She looks at me carefully, then stretches out her index finger and holds it to my face. I don't understand, so she whispers, "E.T., E.T."

I lift my index finger, too, as she gently presses hers against mine until they're joined in the teepee symbol of extraterrestrial life popularized by Steven Spielberg.

"E.T.," she says, and smiles kindly.

Then, she asks me to come closer and whispers into my ear, almost sweetly. "Don't live past seventy. It's hell," and falls back on her pillows.

And so I left deflated. But I was also low because I had come to her house on a pilgrimage of another type. Just minutes before we set out for Kübler-Ross's home in the desert, my husband, Doug, had called long-distance from Toronto. From the first sound of his hushed voice, I knew that something was very wrong. The doctor had just called to tell him that his father was likely to die in the next twenty-four hours. Doug was three hours away from him, and I was at least twelve hours from both of them, and that was only if I cancelled the rest of my interviews in Arizona and started back to Canada immediately.

Death is so jarring, so sad, even when the ailing person is ninety years old—like Doug's dad—and feels almost ready to go. I was especially worried, though, because my husband is an only child who lost his mother to breast cancer when he was young. It was a wretched passing that shadowed him for years. I couldn't bear the possibility that he might face his father's death alone, especially with all that it could summon from the past.

So, driving away from my interview with Kübler-Ross, I couldn't ignore the irony that, as precious minutes ticked by in my father-in-law's life, I had been sitting with an expert in insight who had offered none, with a psychiatrist who had obviously tired of her medical duty of compassion. Here I was dreading death and all she wanted to do was die. "He's lucky," she'd growled when I mentioned my worries.

I called the airline and in tears I managed to get a flight back to Toronto immediately. A friend picked me up from the airport and sped several hours through the night to get me to my husband's side.

And that's when it struck me: I had travelled thousands of miles hoping for insight into surviving life's challenges and living to the fullest, and had found none. Yet at home I had already interviewed dozens of people who'd never published books or received honorary degrees, but whose advice about survival was just as sound, if not more so. The young boy who'd been adopted by alcoholics and kidnapped by pedophiles, but today has nothing but praise for life; the chef who was paralyzed in a terrible car accident, but defied those who told him to abandon his passion; the young mother diagnosed with colon cancer, and given just six months to live, who chose to savour every extra moment.

That night I realized I had learned more about life from these so-called "ordinary people" and had witnessed more courage and conviction in their presence than I'd found in the Arizona desert.

I was sorry for Elisabeth Kübler-Ross's suffering, especially after she'd helped ease the pain of others, and I understood that she had simply had enough. But I was also grateful to her for teaching me—however inadvertently—that we need not make long pilgrimages in search of inspirational life lessons, because our greatest teachers may be our friends, our family members, our colleagues, or even someone we meet on the bus.

And as I rushed to find my husband and hold him as his father passed away, it was the wisdom of these extraordinary "ordinary" people that stayed in my heart.

Goodwood, Canada
2004

A Quiet Courage

DR. GRAEME CUNNINGHAM

Dr. Graeme Cunningham remembers with equal emotional pain both the first time and the last time he took a drink. But he insists he owes everything in his life to alcoholism.

THE SMALL SECOND-FLOOR FLAT in Glasgow has a blue rug and blue wallpaper with pink flowers. On top of the piano there is a silver tray etched with a thistle. There are five crystal glasses on the tray. In a moment, Graeme Cunningham will lift the heavy bottle and pour Johnny Walker Red Label into a glass. His date, a young woman with a cap on her right front tooth, is watching. He is sixteen years old. It will be his first drink and he will never forget it. His father, a local doctor, is a violent drunk who falls in the back door after the pub closes and beats his mother in the morning. In another moment, Cunningham will swallow the first hot gulp of whisky and spend the next twenty-seven years as a drunk. As he lifts the glass to his lips he is thinking, 'This is not too smart. This is the stuff that makes my old man drunk.'

But he wonders, too, what it feels like, what it tastes like, and why it means more to his father than anything or anyone else—including his own son. "I took it, but I know now I was genetically waiting for that drink. And I got an intense reward that I never forgot. That drink filled up all of my soul. It made me feel inside the way folks looked at me outside: put together. It gave me confidence."

Flash forward now to a time almost three decades later. Dr. Graeme Cunningham, a respected specialist in internal medicine in a northern Ontario town, is sitting behind his neatly organized desk with a patient's chart in his hand. At that moment, he snaps out of a drunken haze. He is shocked to find a man sitting in front of him, staring expectantly. He looks down and sees the medical chart, but he does not recognize it. He does not recall picking it up. He can't remember coming to work. And he does not recognize this patient in his office.

When he reaches back for memory, he finds only a New Year's Eve party two full days earlier and an icy gulp of cold beer sliding down his throat.

It's not as if he hasn't blacked out before. He likes to joke that he breaks out in spots after drinking binges—spots like Chicago, Winnipeg, Buffalo. It isn't unusual for him to wake up in his own bed and not remember how he got home or where he left the car.

But this time is different. He's lost two entire days, during which—who knows?—he may have done anything: performed surgery, smashed up his car, left his wife? He is forty-three years old, a father, husband and respected doctor—and he has no idea where he has been for the last forty-eight hours. He feels very frightened. Telling his assistant to cancel his appointments, he leaves the office. It is a bitterly cold day in Timmins, but he strides outside, a tightly built man with no coat and the fair skin of his

Scottish ancestors. His tears rise in steam. He has finally had a moment of clarity. He has seen his alcoholism.

Remembering that winter day, Cunningham says, "I felt tremendous panic and fear. I had seen myself the way people in my life must have seen me, my wives, my staff, my kids. And I knew at that point, very clearly, that if I didn't do something, I was going to die.

"I think all of us have moments where we say 'This can't go on.' This moment of sanity, this realization that I have to change, that the problem isn't my wife, the job, the boss, the kids. I am the problem."

Despite what we hear about addicts' need to "hit bottom" before they are willing to face their problems, Cunningham believes "the bottom can be brought up to you." For the doctor it wasn't just one particularly outrageous bout of boozing, but dozens of near-tragic episodes that culminated in the realization that his madness must end.

Graeme Cunningham grew up in Glasgow, Scotland, the eldest son of a family doctor. It wasn't until he was ten years old, though, that he allowed himself to understand that his "respectable" if violent father was a "problem drinker," plagued by an insidious disease that would strip him of money and respect, and eventually take his life. Graeme's mother, a timid and proper woman, kept the house and her husband's secret. "He was a severe alcoholic. Died of it and lost everything, but it was hushed up, just pushed under the rug," he says.

From the outside, the house Graeme shared with his parents and two siblings appeared orderly. Inside, chaos reigned. "It was violent. It was abusive. It was dangerous. It was dishonest. It was awful."

Most days, he and his younger brother and sister would awake to find their father cranky and hung over, still in bed. By the time they returned from school, he'd be back from work and drunk again or off at the pub. Well after their dinner, he'd bang through the back door and lunge at his wife. If the boy tried to protect his mother, which he did increasingly, his father would pummel him with his fists or whip him with a belt.

Perhaps worse, though, were the mother-son fireside chats that bordered on emotional incest.

"I was my mother's surrogate husband. She would share her feelings with me. She would tell me about her suicide plans. We would sit at night and discuss my dad's drinking with all kinds of helpless, hopeless feelings. And he'd be in bed, drunk."

Graeme was thirteen years old.

Six years later, he tried to kill his father, and almost succeeded. Pent-up rage burst from his fists. "I punched him and knocked him down. He struck his head on the edge of a small coffee table and was knocked out and I grabbed him by the throat and I literally would have throttled him to death if my brother hadn't pulled me off."

His mother stood behind her drunken husband and pleaded with her son to leave him alone. "Think of your career."

She wanted him to be a doctor, like his father.

For too long, he would be.

There are scenes from our lives we never forget. For Cunningham, it was his grandmother taking him aside after the melee. "A little, wise old Scottish lady. She hugged me, and she said: 'Some day this will all make sense.'

"But my feelings were feelings of being let down, being left alone and being abandoned and put into a role I should never have been put into, and how that manifested in me was rage. And it took me years to work through that."

As so often happens when a child experiences conflict, young Cunningham imagined himself as its cause. For years, he could think of only one explanation for his father's behaviour. "This is my fault. The message throughout my formative years was: You're not good enough. If you were, your father wouldn't be a drunk."

It wouldn't be the only way his father failed him. On his own much of the time, Cunningham looked for others to emulate. One man took an interest in him and invited him home to chat. Then the man stripped and bathed him. "It felt yicky. I just didn't like it." He told his father, the doctor, about the sordid bath. But the doctor did nothing more than forbid him to go near the man again. "It wasn't until I became an adult and began to look at my life in general that I realized that was an abusive relationship with a person in a position of power."

And that brought to two the number of Cunningham's male role models and the number who'd let him down.

Certain that the only way to save his family and himself was to become a perfect child, Cunningham unleashed a powerful drive, fuelled by anger. He studied and practised and worked and competed, in class and on the field in soccer and rugby. He won scholarships and trophies and made it into medical school at seventeen; later, in Canada, he joined the Masonic Lodge and became president of the Shriners. A joiner, an overachiever, a show-off.

"I was very competitive and very aggressive. I think I was trying to improve my ego. I was an egomaniac with an inferiority complex." But none of the glory managed to replace the fundamental love and respect he couldn't find at home. "It was always empty. It was always hollow."

Except when he filled it up with drink.

Medical school, far from rescuing him, had introduced him to a host of new drinking buddies, who especially loved to finish a rugby match in a pool of liquor. And while he didn't see it for decades, his alcoholism probably cost him a medical career in the United Kingdom.

"I think alcohol was already clouding my judgment and my decision-making. When I was twenty-three, I failed an examination for the very first time in my life." He hadn't been drinking the day of the specialist exam in internal medicine, but he'd been indulging heavily during his training and study. "I think my focus, my drive, my commitment, was a bit lax and was being affected by alcohol."

Cunningham took the test again and passed, but began to look around for a posting where he could start fresh, without the doubt now surrounding him. When he told his supervising professor he'd located a position in Canada, there was no attempt to keep him or cure him. He remembers his supervisor saying simply that it was a good idea. "So, I think he was aware by that time I was having some difficulties."

Cunningham would run into that professor at a Glasgow medical conference twenty years later. "I see you don't drink any more," he commented.

To this day that disturbs Cunningham. "That man had some insight into my difficulty way back in the 1960s and early '70s and didn't say anything."

Except advising him to take his problem elsewhere?

"Yeah," Cunningham says. "Go drink Canada dry."

Just because someone older or wiser sees your problem and does nothing it doesn't mean nothing should be done.

In 1970, Cunningham joined a respectable family practice in Parry Sound, Ontario. Three years later, he moved to Toronto for specialist training and became the chief resident at a prominent teaching hospital in the city.

But bigger professional opportunities also gave Cunningham access to cocaine, lots of it, on the ear, nose and throat trays in the emergency department, and from certain colleagues who had well-supplied street connections. Not only was "coke" available in Toronto in the mid-seventies, he admits there was acceptance of drug use among some medical practitioners.

"I hung out with the guys that drank a bit and used drugs, because that was where I was comfortable."

On a work day, he'd start drinking around three o'clock and consume at least a twenty-six-ounce bottle of whisky before popping two or three sedatives, usually Valium, so he could sleep at night. On the weekends, he started earlier.

"I don't think I was ever addicted to cocaine in the true sense. I liked the way it felt but it wasn't terribly important to me, whereas alcohol was. Alcohol is my drug of choice."

What does a doctor with the equivalent of twenty-six drinks in his bloodstream and countless grams of cocaine up his nose act like?

"There are only three or four chief residents in the city in any given year. It's usually an appointment given to someone who's identified as being bright, capable and responsible. So that's presumably how I acted—bright and capable and responsible."

But he was also trapped. "There was always a little voice that said, 'You don't know what you are doing. You're a scumbag. So no matter what you achieve, you don't deserve it.'"

The greater Cunningham's lack of confidence, the greater his need to drink to hide it; the more he drank, the less respect he had for himself and the lower his confidence—and the greater his need to drink. He drew his own vicious circle and coloured it in.

He learned to buy square rather than round bottles, so they wouldn't roll around when he hid them under the seat in his car. And he pushed people away. "The alcoholic in the SkyDome who wants to drink from his mickey will go to the washroom, into the stall, and close and lock the door. Utterly alone with 50,000 people around them. That's what addiction does."

At home, Cunningham kept a "cocktail cabinet" and became a wine connoisseur, although today he believes he was just a wino with a chequebook. "So I had a wine cellar and I drank an awful lot of pink, frothy, immature wine, reflecting my own immaturity to some extent."

At the office, Cunningham says he broke his oath. "When a patient enters a physician's office, there's the assumption that they're safe and the doctor is sober. Did I breach that by being hung over? Yes, to my eternal shame, I breached that unique contract. It was never my intention. I went to medical school to be the best doctor I could be. Instead, I became a drunk doctor."

The closest Cunningham believes he came to disaster was the night he was in the operating room after drinking. "A colleague called me at home wanting help to put in a pacemaker. So I came in and did it. And I was drunk."

The procedure was a success and Cunningham showed up the next morning expecting kudos from his colleagues. Instead, "everyone just went quiet and didn't talk," he recalls.

Somewhere, it registered in Cunningham's mind that they knew he'd been drunk and disapproved, but "I was a senior physician and people were perhaps reluctant to speak to me for that reason or maybe, because I was arrogant and difficult to get along with, people didn't confront me about those things in case I blew up at them."

It never occurred to him to confront himself. "That didn't register on my consciousness. What did register was the fact that I did a good job. And so the ego kicked in and said, 'Boy, you did a hell of a good job there.'"

He understands now that a social drinker would have explained that he'd had a couple of drinks and begged off. But the alcoholic doctor, the man who needs to be needed, squeezes drops into his eyes, sprays breath freshener and pops on his surgical mask: "You need me? I get in there. And you hide the illness. It's a disease of shame; it's a disease of guilt.

"Some of us doctors think 'MD' stands for 'malignant denial' and I had a lot of malignant denial for a long time.

"The important point is, once alcoholism shows up in a doctor's practice, it's always very advanced because they can hide it so well. They're highly trained. Now if I'd been asked to sweep the floors rather than put in a pacemaker, maybe my alcoholism would have shown up a lot earlier. I wasn't trained to sweep the floor, but I sure as heck was trained to put in pacemakers."

Meanwhile, Cunningham had lost one seven-year marriage to his erratic behaviour and was actively jeopardizing his second. "I wasn't violent. I knew how abhorrent and inappropriate *that* was. But I still was an inconsistent, unpredictable individual with significant mood swings, who a lot of the time just wasn't around."

His new wife, Linda, a nurse, would go to work at night and leave him to babysit their young children. Once, he was so drunk while changing his son's diaper that he staggered backward and grabbed for the change table, knocking it over. Miraculously, he managed to scoop up the baby before he fell to the floor.

Again, although he felt a stab of fear, he "denied and minimized" it. Mainly, he felt happy he'd caught the baby and relieved his wife hadn't been home to witness the event. "Now, many years later, I look back in horror, but at the time it didn't register."

One of his biggest regrets is that his two oldest children from his first marriage, a son and a daughter, didn't have the father they deserved. "I often lose sleep over this to this day, how I didn't support them the way a dad should have."

Sober, Cunningham looks back with fresh pain, the pain his drinking obscured. He now remembers his young son packing up his hockey bag and heading out—alone—into the early morning dark. He never once saw his boy play an "away" game. "The kid would go and play hockey and his dad wouldn't watch."

Cunningham, the absent father, always had an excuse. Too much work and being "terribly busy." The truth? "Hung over. Not wanting to get along with the parents. Social isolation. Leave me alone."

Just as his father had neglected him, he neglected his son.

Now, Cunningham is deeply grateful for that fateful post-New Year's blackout, because it led to his recovery. "Finally, I just had this really clear realization that I was in desperate trouble."

Cunningham had great medical connections, of course, and checked into an addiction treatment centre immediately. He took his last drink on the way, and left the bottle on the floor of the cab.

For all his medical training, finding a way out of addiction proved more daunting than he'd ever imagined, because it meant facing an unpleasant truth: Dr. Graeme Cunningham was a big fat liar.

"I think the essence of addiction is that you live a lie. To this day, lying is sometimes easier for me than telling the truth.

"Folks blame alcohol for alcoholism. But my problem wasn't alcohol, my problem was sobriety. I couldn't stand being sober. Sober stands for, excuse the language, 'Son of a bitch! The thing's real.' And it's the reality that bothers me because I didn't fit in. I'm not quite good enough. And the alcohol took all those inadequate feelings away."

> *Until you admit you own your addiction and*
> *must reform, you can't own a solution.*

He'd grown up in a house of secrets, where his father's alcoholism and then his own were coddled and concealed. "You close the front door and you pull the wagons around. You won't share your weakness or your own inabilities with anyone."

In addition to the deceit he'd learned to practise, Cunningham says he also suffered from what he calls "terminal uniqueness"—the belief, stoked by alcohol, that he was better than anyone. "It's the egomaniac mixed with an inferiority complex. When I was feeling less secure I would be the arrogant doctor, in charge and in control. So the outside did not fairly reflect the inside."

That "false" superiority gave him permission to ignore social rules. "Why shouldn't I speed on the highway? Why do I need to stop at an amber light?" More importantly, his sense of omnipotence tricked him, time and again, into thinking he could take just one drink and stop. When he first heard about the new line of "light" alcoholic beverages, the coolers and the spritzers, his "terminal uniqueness" persona convinced him he could handle them. "My experience when I began drinking alcohol, though, was that I couldn't guarantee the outcome. Once I start, it's the first drink that gets me drunk, not the tenth or the twentieth. So I don't pick up the first drink."

It was shock and fear that brought Cunningham to treatment, but in the end it was simple honesty that saved him. Cut off from his bottle, stripped of authority and housed with the rest of the clients in the clinic, the doctor finally "gave up." He still remembers the date—January 14, 1986—when he knelt and prayed to a tree.

"I got down on my knees by my bed in the room and talked to a large fir tree outside. I said something like, 'I am frightened. I don't know if I can do this. I need help.'"

Then, he climbed into bed and says he had the best sleep in years. "What I was doing that night, looking back, was just giving up, surrendering." Cunningham believes that was the key to his success.

Just surrender? It's an unusual theory in a world that prizes fighters, but Cunningham, who now counsels addicts, says he's seen the evidence in himself and in the patients he's helped.

"Society says we've got to *fight* illness, fight cancer, fight heart disease. But if you fight addiction, you'll always lose. If you give up, surrender, then paradoxically, you start to win."

If you fight addiction, you'll lose.

That's because addiction is always stronger than willpower, he says. "And you won't beat it until you surrender to the fact that you are ill and unable to do anything about it without treatment or help from a higher power."

Surrender to the fact you are ill.

Addiction is a disease that will whip you in an arm-wrestle, and suck all the strength out of your limbs as it does. The more you fight, the stronger it gets, the harder you have to fight. Battling only gives it a bigger victory over you when you fail.

It is a devious disease, fuelled by both the physiological need for an addictive substance and the psychological comfort being supplied by the addiction. There is an addiction to the drug, and there is an addiction to its effect. In other words, despite its many costs, addiction supplies something of value to the addict—in Cunningham's case, ego gratification and escape.

So to extract himself from the grip of alcoholism, Cunningham had to do more than just stop drinking. He had to eliminate those aspects of his life and of his personality that were dependent upon alcohol, that were succoured by drink. He had to stop hiding from his true self and learn to live—sober—with the pain of human life.

And he had to deflate that massive ego that had hardened like scar tissue around the broken heart of a little boy whose father had abandoned him. "False pride must go. Ego deflation must occur. You really need to start looking at yourself, rather that at everyone else."

When the doctor awoke from his "night of surrender," he says he felt "different." To this day, Cunningham—who'd never been at home in the strict Presbyterian Church of his youth—believes part of surrendering was opening his mind to the possibility of a power greater than himself. He won't take credit for finally deciding to pull himself out of alcoholism. "I didn't. It was God, as I understand God in a personal sense. He said it's time now."

Over the next few days, the compulsion to drink began to slip away. "What I used to call my 'cold wind blowing through the middle' that only a four-finger measure of brown Scottish liquid would take away. That had gone."

When Cunningham put down the bottle, sat still and screwed up his courage to look inside, guess what he found?

Anger, of course, but its depth—and duration—stunned him.

Over the years, long after he'd kicked alcohol, Cunningham continued to seek out different therapies, including a psychodrama program in Tennessee where participants re-enact the violence in their lives. In Cunningham's tableau, four actors played past persecutors. He became so enraged that, at one point, he pulled them and the big chesterfield upon which they all sat clear across the room. It helped.

He still uses a technique he invented himself to drain his frustration. He gets in the car on the highway, with the windows rolled up, and he screams. Or he goes into the bush and yells at the trees until the churning force inside him is spent. "Because if I don't let it out, it'll come out in other ways. It will come out in secrets or unhealthy behaviours or negative attitudes, like criticism and judgmentalism. These are the warning flags that I have to talk to somebody."

Don't collect negative feelings.

It's been more than eighteen years since Graeme Cunningham took his last drink, although, as with all addicts, it's been one step at a time. He thinks about drinking every single day, not the whisky so much as his long journey through alcoholism and his continuing campaign of recovery.

"Every morning I get up and the first thing I do is pray. I say, 'Give me the strength to stay sober today.' I'm not quite sure who I am talking to, but I do it because I was told to do it and it works."

Before he starts work, the doctor then spends about thirty minutes in his office, reading spiritual and inspirational books, and taking some quiet time. He asks himself how he can apply what he's just read to the day ahead.

At night, once the family is tucked in, he reflects for a few more minutes before going to bed and asks himself when during the day he was selfish, dishonest, resentful or frightened. And he decides whether he needs to make adjustments or apologies.

Cunningham says he will forever be working on his character "defects"—dishonesty, inflexibility, the need to control, the desire to always be better than others. He knows that they are the weapons he forged when he was a mistreated child; but he has no excuse for carrying that arsenal today.

Once a man with little emotional sensitivity, he has evolved into one who pays attention to feelings first. "Because I can't let those things fester. The emotional abscesses would come back and I'd want to pour some chemicals on them."

He is very careful, too, to maintain strong, honest friendships. Besides his wife of more than two decades, from whom he keeps no secrets, there have been four critically important men in his life; three of them priests. He's told them what he considers to be every awful detail of his character. The fact they still love and support him helps him peel away the feelings of worthlessness.

"I can very easily go on a pity pot if I want to. It's not a comfortable place to be. If I'm on it, key people in my life will say: 'You're on the pity pot, get off.'"

To counteract this self-centredness, which Cunningham says is just another way to justify giving in to destructive behaviour, he writes his Gratitude List. "I'm grateful I am alive. I'm grateful I'm sober. I'm grateful my eyes work. I'm grateful I can hear. I am grateful I have family. It's amazing how long the list gets." And he puts that thankfulness into action by sending his wife flowers or giving his mother a telephone call.

Get off your pity pot.

Cunningham believes it must have been heartbreaking for his mother to watch both her husband and then her son succumb to alcoholism. At seventeen, he'd come home late from the pub, just as his father did, and his mother would say nothing. "I would come home intoxicated, but I was living in a home of secrets. I was living in a home of silence." She has never mentioned his alcoholism, or its likely origin, in a quarter century. It is only very recently that Cunningham talked to her about his disease, and discussed what she could do to help herself deal with the effects of all those years. Does she understand? No. Has she done anything about it? No.

"I found it frustrating for a while. I would get angry and then very sad. I would ask her, 'Why won't you see what I was doing? That I was making the same mistake?' But she's still got her own issues and difficulties, which she'll not resolve because nothing's changed. You know, the drinkers are no longer in the house, but the memories are still there."

Some people, including family members,
will fail to resolve their own issues before
they die, let alone help you with yours.

It is no accident that Cunningham has emerged from his struggle to become one of the most respected experts in the field of addiction counselling and treatment. He is currently the director of the addiction division of the well-respected Homewood Health Centre in Guelph, Ontario, and an associate professor of psychiatry at McMaster University in Hamilton. In 2003, he had the honour of serving as president of the Ontario College of Physicians and Surgeons, the body that, among other things, monitors and disciplines physicians.

In that post, he spent a great deal of time helping addicted doctors admit their illness and find help. Doing that work has helped ease his resentment of his father's behaviour.

"Part of recovering from an addiction is a process of forgiveness. You forgive yourself in the context of forgiving other people. A lot of us grew up with problems. I was sexually abused. I was physically abused. I can rail and rant against perpetrators until the end of my life. What's the point? We live in a victim society and I think that's sad."

He admits to feeling sorry for himself from time to time—"Just ask my wife!"—but strongly resists the urge to blame anyone. "When there's a finger pointing at somebody else, there are three fingers pointing back at you. It's much easier to blame than to say, 'What's my role in this, what's my place or what do I need to change about myself?' That's far harder. I think that's the reason we don't do that in society now, because this process takes hard work."

Blaming someone else for your troubles
puts a solution out of your reach.

But ultimately, how do you put right the injustice done to a small boy who was robbed of his childhood? No child deserves that. "It wasn't a matter of deserving. Those were just the facts," Cunningham says. "If one accepts that and then asks 'What was my role in it?' you see your role was no role. You do not need to take any responsibility. Then you can forgive yourself in the process."

In fact, Cunningham is beyond forgiveness; incredibly, he's even thankful for what's happened to him.

"It's given me the opportunity to change and try to be the best physician in terms of interacting with people. So that crisis, that chaos, has given me a gift—the chance to be committed and to be focused and to be reliable and to be predictable now."

Yet surely we do not need to endure crisis to grow emotionally? Surviving the hellfires of alcoholism or loss or illness seems too high a price for anyone to pay. Think of all the time Cunningham wasted, wandering in a drunken stupor, numbing himself to avoid experiencing the real events of his life.

"There's another way of looking at it," Cunningham says. "Everything I have today is *because* of alcoholism. Because of my recovery from alcoholism. Without alcoholism, I don't even think I would be alive. So out of that chaos, out of that craziness, has come everything I have today."

Ask yourself: What is the gift in this crisis?

Cunningham's personal journey required enormous courage and insight—a forced emotional evolution. "My most tragic defect has become my biggest asset."

The skills he developed to survive became those that enable him to thrive.

"To be the accepted, comfortable, caring human being I am now, I had to have been alienated, bewildered, despairing and demoralized. I had to go through those things to get to the place I'm at now. So I don't see those years as bad years. I see them as part of a journey. That people were bruised and damaged is part of that journey. I'm very sorry for that and I've made amends as best I can, but it's still part of the journey."

He understands why some people in his life worry he might slip back into the clutches of addiction. Just as he knows that words alone can never again reassure those who've been betrayed. "But if I am consistent, predictable and honest, there is no reason for concern."

Today, Cunningham lives his life "spiritually." He jokes that religious people fear hell, while spiritual people have been there. To him, being spiritual means being honest. "The home I grew up in was a total lie, and I lived a total lie. Then I left home and continued to live lies. So it's been easy for me when stressed or under pressure to slip back into being less than honest. I continue to struggle with that."

And he works to minimize resentment.

"Resentment comes from the Latin verb *resentire*—to feel again. When you do something bad to me, what my head does is replay the events and *you* get worse and *I* get better. Then, you end up living rent-free up there in the dangerous neighbourhood called my mind. I deal with that by becoming selfish."

It's an emotional pattern laid down early, which Cunningham says he must always guard against.

And to stay happy, he must stay connected to things that make him feel good about himself in a *healthy* way—the love of friends and family, good music, nature, a well-hit golf shot—"These are the things that just make the insides feel the way the outsides look."

So, when his tiny Scottish grandmother took him aside and hugged him and told him that one day it would all make sense, she was right.

"My father wasn't an evil man. He was a sick man. He was a doctor who couldn't cure himself. I can certainly understand that."

MARY BROWN

She lost her beloved mother in a car accident and her husband to cocaine. Then she was diagnosed with terminal cancer. And that was when she learned how to truly live.

I T STARTED WITH THE FLU. At least, she figured it was the flu—or maybe an attack of really bad indigestion after she sampled every dish at the school's holiday potluck. Mary Brown, the vivacious mother of two, recalls the first signs of cancer: "I love food, so I ate and ate, and afterwards I had such a pain in my neck and in my side—to the point of tears." She tried to sleep it off but the ache intensified.

The following day, her doctor suspected trouble with her gall bladder or her liver, which appeared swollen on the ultrasound screen. There were odd shadows, too, so an abdominal scan was ordered, but not scheduled until the new year.

Brown figured the wait meant no one was particularly worried about her "stomach ache." At worst, she suspected she might need surgery. But looking back, "I realize they were probably thinking: 'Have a nice Christmas—it could be your last.'"

It's early January 1996. Brown is sitting in another doctor's office, a day after her scan. The doctor is shaking his head.

"I cannot believe it is you with this diagnosis. I don't like having an afternoon like this, with people like you," he says.

Brown is confused. Like who? Like what? What sort of afternoon is he having?

"Are you saying it's something serious?" Brown asks.

"It's just about as serious as it gets," he says.

Brown has a very good sense of humour, quick and self-deprecating. She laughs. "What, like you think I am going die from this?"

The doctor looks down. "Probably," he says.

Brown pursues him. "Sure, in like six months, six years?"

She doesn't believe a word she is saying or hearing, yet she keeps asking for more.

"More like six months," he answers.

Six months.

Six months to live. She is forty-six years old. Two children. A loving husband. She's right in the middle of a big renovation project at work. She's a sales manager in the accessories department at Eaton's, the Toronto department store, and she's been putting in twelve-hour days. Breathing, living, loving for just six more months. How many days is that?

Six times thirty. One hundred and eighty.

The word cancer is not mentioned in that doctor's office, and won't be, until a biopsy is performed. But there are tumours in Brown's liver, and it's likely they're the result of cancer that's metastasized from another part of her body. Glowing, beautiful and vibrant on the outside, Brown is being slowly eaten alive inside.

Brown is angry with the doctor on this January day. She doesn't like the way he's treating her, but she says nothing. Instead, she tries to imagine how difficult it must be to deliver such deadly news. She makes excuses for him. Perhaps he is trying to be gentle and compassionate, but he hasn't gone through that experience, and doesn't necessarily know how to handle it.

Still, she is stunned that her specialist would blame her diagnosis for ruining his afternoon.

"Hey," she remembers thinking. "Try being in my place! At first, you're shocked and you're upset. Then, when you look back on it, you think: well, they're just people, they're trying their best and some are better at it than others."

Brown is what we like to call an optimist. But don't conclude she's an emotional simpleton, safely insulated from deep feelings by false cheer. She's suffered bouts of depression, anxiety attacks and old-fashioned fear.

"But I always try to cultivate optimism," she says. "Even when I was young I did that. I just hate that feeling in the pit of your stomach when you're depressed. You're walking along and everything's fine and all of a sudden it just grabs you and you think, 'Ahhhh.' You're so uptight or anxious."

By the time she was in her twenties, Brown had devised a method for fighting her blues. She still uses it.

First, she tries to pinpoint the cause of the depression.

"What is bugging me right now? Let's look at it." Then, she takes the problem, rolls it around in her head, watching the light refract, seeing it from a new perspective. "Is there any good way of looking at this situation?" she asks. "Is there anything positive in this at all? And I cling to that."

From her mother, a nurse, Mary learned to diagnose situations. From her father, an engineer, she learned that "there is a solution to everything. You may not always be able to think of it, but there is a solution."

There is always a solution, although not necessarily devised by you.

So, as a young adult, what might have bothered Brown and how would she have handled it? A guy, for example, who promised to call at 2 p.m. But he's not calling. She waits. She's getting worried and, eventually, upset.

Here's how Brown thinks about the situation. Maybe, she says to herself, he's not calling on time because he is upset with me, or doesn't like me any more. Not a happy thought. So she analyzes it: is there any reason for him to be upset with me? If the answer is yes, she prepares an explanation of her behaviour and motivation and plans to tell him what he needs to know.

But if she is confident she's not in the wrong, she has to think the situation through again. If he's aggravated with her, it must be for no good reason. So, Brown concludes, maybe she doesn't need this person in her life after all. So, it might be a good thing that he's broken his word and hasn't called her as promised. He will either have a good explanation for what happened, or it is a telling clue and he may not be worth having around. "That's fine. Okay. Let's move on."

Or perhaps Brown's family is invited out to a great party but she sprains her ankle and can't go. "I can stay home and mope or I can think, Home alone! I can work on my scrapbook, make myself a nice drink, listen to my favourite music, watch that movie no one else wanted to see, call my friend in Fergus and have a long chat, soak in the tub and read my new book.

"The point is to forget about what you thought was going to happen and start seeing it another way. If you can't change a situation, change the way you look at it. It's not that hard. It just takes practice. Eventually, you do it automatically."

So, in young Mary Brown's books, when a guy doesn't call as he promised, it's not necessarily a bad thing. When a doctor is callous it is not entirely his fault. When people are cruel, they do not always mean it.

You have to love Brown. She'll need that optimism. Life has a lot more in store for her.

Looking back, Brown remembers a "blessed" life. She had great parents, and grew up tall, slim and beautiful, with glossy dark hair—the archetypal "popular girl." Then life got even better. A sexy husband, darling children and a job she loved. But when the calendar flipped to 1989, she says, "all hell broke loose."

First, her brother's long and seemingly happy marriage broke apart, sending shock waves through the close-knit family.

A month later, her father was driving her mother to pick up train tickets for her trip to a fiftieth nursing-school reunion. It's unclear exactly what happened, she says, but as they were turning left, another car slammed into the passenger side, and her energetic, beloved mother died on her way to hospital. Brown's father was left in critical condition, just "a human mass that drooled and picked things out of the air."

Shortly afterward, a family member whispered that she believed Brown's husband, Max, had a cocaine problem.

It seemed impossible. Every night Brown would visit her father in the hospital while her husband made dinner for their children. He would join her later at the hospital, loving and supportive. "When somebody's first on cocaine, they've got a lot of energy and they're just wonderful," she says.

Brown could barely manage the grief already on her plate, so she rebuffed her relative's concerns. But the doubt had been planted. She began to notice money trickling inexplicably from their bank account, along with lost hours during the day when she couldn't account for her husband's whereabouts. She could no longer avoid accepting the truth. "I became incredibly good at telling whether he'd taken any drugs that day."

Just as Brown would never chastise her callous cancer doctor, it took her months and months to confront her husband. She said nothing, and instead, hung her heart on his addiction. "I would allow my day to be up and down depending on whether he was doing drugs or not. As soon as I'd find he hadn't been around for a couple of hours at work, I'd crash down again."

She told herself cocaine was just like a few extra drinks to Max. It calmed his frazzled nerves after a high-pressure day running his own business. After all, she reasoned, he could handle his liquor, and he was always a funny drunk. So how could it really be a problem? And his business, the typesetting company he'd set up on his own, was foundering, so how could she blame him for needing a release for his stress?

Eventually, Brown dragged Max to therapy, trying to finesse a solution. But Max dropped out quickly, insisting he could kick his habit on his own.

Ironically, it was Brown, who'd begun therapy for her husband's sake and was certain she "wasn't doing anything wrong," who stayed with the therapy. She had realized that she was in trouble herself.

The diagnosis? Mary had a case of terminal niceness. "Mary, you get what you settle for," her therapist had told her repeatedly. "You're biting your tongue, you're holding back comments. I know you're thinking these things, Mary. You've got to say them. You've got to be more forthright. You've got to stand up for yourself more."

You get what you settle for.

She started doing her own research, and when she read the description of an "enabler"—wanting to get along with everyone, never making waves so people would like her—she recognized herself.

Her therapist wasn't the only one to see the problem. "One of my friends gave me a book that said people like me need to get in touch with their inner 'bitch.' She was only half joking," Brown says.

It was difficult, though, for Brown to change: she can't even pronounce the word 'bitch' without blushing. She'd been raised as a "good girl," whose politeness was encouraged and whose co-operation was rewarded, mainly by her mother.

"Perhaps it is generational, or about women in general or the way your family works. I do not know, but I know my mother always tried to make things nice, too," Brown says. "We would always talk about 'smoothing the tablecloth,' because I can remember sitting at the dining-room table so many nights and if people were arguing or whatever, my mother would be trying to placate them, smoothing out all the wrinkles in the tablecloth. That's what she taught me and that's sort of our analogy, of always trying to keep it smooth."

Unlike Mary, her oldest brother didn't hold back, particularly when it came to differences with their father. So, mother and daughter would work hard to "smooth the tablecloth over" disputes between father and son. "Everybody's fine," they would say. "Everybody's happy. Dad really wants you to do this, or your son just meant that, or he isn't really angry."

Brown's therapist helped her discover that she was excessively nice because she believed it was her job to maintain the status quo, no matter how crippling it was. She *had* to avoid change, even if it meant compromising herself because she saw change as a threat.

"There are many instances in your life where your integrity has been jeopardized. I didn't do anything about it. I've always wanted to smooth everything over and make it nice and I'd go away thinking 'How dare they say such a thing to me?' But I didn't say anything about it. Those are the things that are hard for me— and I think for a lot of people: learning how to say something to the person at the time it's happening, without making it a big huge thing."

Max was in for a surprise, too, one Brown says was long overdue. After thirteen years of marriage, two kids and an addiction that had brought them to the brink of disaster, Mary Brown began to stand up to her husband. She finally faced the destructive cycle that had plagued her entire marriage: she'd point out a concern, then back away, smothering her unhappiness. With her therapist to keep her on track, she pinpointed the moment at which the problem started between them.

It was while they were dating, happily. Brown was taking night classes at Ryerson University in Toronto. Every day after class, Max always picked her up. Except the night he didn't. She waited ten, twenty minutes. No Max. Brown stood fuming on the darkened street, passed by panhandlers and eyed by pimps. Almost an hour later, Max showed up. He'd been at the pub with friends and couldn't tear himself away. Mary was mad, and told him so. "You needed that extra fifty minutes with them? How many hours had you already been there?"

But two days later, she acted as if nothing had happened. Mad Mary gone; Nice Mary back. After that, "things just got maddening . . . and I let them." Today, more than anything, Brown regrets "settling" for Max's inconsiderate behaviour so early in their relationship. It didn't help her and it didn't help him.

"If I had said to him that night, 'If you ever do this again I won't be there the next time'—and meant it—it would have stopped. There's a whole pattern of having to learn to do that. To have enough self-respect to stand up for yourself."

Have enough self-respect to stand up for yourself.

It was this lesson, perhaps more than any other, that would help Brown save her marriage, take control of her own cancer care, and make a tremendous difference in the lives of the cancer patients she now counsels.

Like many "nice" people, Brown could be pushed to a breaking point, albeit an extremely distant one, way off on the horizon, past the mountains of anger and the wide skies of swallowed resentment. Once she'd reached that point, though, she would stand her ground. With her burgeoning self-esteem and a supportive therapist who urged her to speak more truthfully, Brown had finally had enough of Max, who was seesawing with cocaine addiction, stopping and starting again, stopping and starting.

She confronted him. "What is more important than these children?" she demanded. "What sensation, thrill, comfort, could matter more than doing the right thing for this family?"

Max stood silent. There seemed to be no answer, she told him, but divorce. The next morning, though, he asked her to give him two weeks; if he could make it through, he'd know he had quit. And he did it. They would need each other in the years to come, embattled by debt and, finally, cancer. But Brown now had the partner she should have demanded far earlier. In the secure environment of therapy, Brown says she realized that what she feared most—change—was actually inevitable, and that it was, in fact, the only thing we *can* count on in life.

"It would be hideously boring without change," she says today. "Change brings you lessons, and you will get the same lesson over and over until you get it."

The lesson will repeat itself until you learn it.

Lessons—seeing benefits in bad luck, the good side of gloomy days—had been Brown's specialty since youth, so the pieces began to make sense for her.

What lessons were tragedy and uninvited, unwanted change trying to teach her? Or, less mystically, what benefit, what learning could she wring from the pain of losing her beloved mother and watching her father suffer—or from seeing her husband crumble and her well-to-do lifestyle evaporate?

"The main thing for me is security. My security was in my parents and in money, and in two or three years it was all gone. You sort of feel like an orphan after your parents die, even at forty. The sense is that there's no home to move back to, you're on your own, you've got to make enough money."

For Brown, "being alone" was the life lesson she needed most, one she is convinced she'd never have had the strength to face without the impetus of tragedy. From pain, through pain, to survive pain, Brown forged her independence. She survived loss, her husband's addiction, bereavement and financial ruin. Rather than see those setbacks as debilitating, even paralyzing, she now saw that they would make her stronger. By choosing to stand up on her own, by choosing to face her problems, rather than crumbling and relying on someone else, Brown gave herself a gift: the ability not just to survive but to thrive—in the face of adversity, *because of* adversity.

Mary Brown found herself in her early forties and on her own. Her parents' support was gone. Her husband was a recovering drug addict. Their business was bankrupt. All the tablecloth-smoothing smiles and charm in the world weren't going to turn life around. Carefully, she considered her predicament. The house was mortgaged to the hilt to cover the bankrupt company's bills; their real estate investments had turned sour and were sucking up money now rather than paying out. They needed money, but they had nowhere to turn. Business consultants suggested they declare bankruptcy and leave their creditors holding the bag. Max refused to do that, which made Brown very proud of him. But how would they survive?

Night after night, for months, Brown battled sweats and a racing pulse as anxiety attacks swept through her in waves. She fell asleep searching for a solution and awoke in a depression.

She wasn't a quitter, never had been. But now she had no one to depend on but herself. She could succumb or, accepting that life is change and that agonizing change can produce powerful results, she could act. But she would have to give up on idealistic expectations that all would be provided for her, or that security lay elsewhere. Perhaps that's why life had become so intolerably painful—to galvanize her into action.

And then one day, when these ideas had sufficiently coalesced, Brown had an epiphany: "I just woke up and thought, *Sell the house.* Sell the house, pay it all off and start again. Because otherwise we would owe money for years.

"The moment I thought that, it was total relief. It was like, 'Yeah, so what? You start over again! Big deal.'" The panic attacks eased. No longer waiting for someone else to take control—and terrified because her traditional rescuers were gone—Brown seized control herself. She was, after all, the one person she could count on, the only person over whom she really had control. "I knew what my standards were and how to meet them. I knew what had to be done to make me feel comfortable. I was the very best person in the world to take care of myself."

You can control only one person: Yourself.

Over time, as Brown changed, the dynamics within her family changed too. In the past, when Max and her children had argued, Brown had immediately intervened. Now she discovered that everyone got along better if she didn't step in. "'You know what, you don't like what he's doing, you tell him. It's not bothering me. *You* tell him.' And it felt great. You know? I am not responsible for my children's behaviour all the time. I am not responsible for whether they get along with people all the time. Like, have fun. Let's be who we are."

Five years later, almost free of the anchor of debt, Brown was working full time at Eaton's, the kids were happy and Max was drug free.

And then Mary Brown got the "flu" and was told she had six months to live.

"I had come through enough stuff in the last ten years, and I thought surely to goodness God's not going to kill me off with cancer now. I know you like to be ironic up there, but this is a bit much."

So certain were the doctors of Brown's imminent demise that they offered her intense chemotherapy immediately, to buy her a little time. But they also suggested that she mainly prepare for palliative care—pain relief for the final stages of terminal cancer. Incredulous that this could be happening to *her*, Brown researched her condition like a rabid doctoral student. The medical research backed up what the doctors were saying.

But by now good-girl Mary Brown was a far tougher person as a result of her earlier struggles. Her backbone was steel. She grabbed at chemotherapy immediately and began to haunt a different section of her library, reading not medical texts, but anything she could find on spiritual healing. "What other kind of healing can there be? There must be something else," she told herself.

In the meantime, she ignored her cancer as best she could, continuing to work full time, telling no one but her boss about the death sentence she'd received, and quietly slipping out for chemotherapy on her lunch breaks.

Oh, Norma, I'm off for a sandwich and a radioactive cocktail. Can I bring you back anything?

She went for treatment every day for four days, then took the fifth and most debilitating day off from work. These once-a-month cycles continued for eighteen months.

"I'd feel crummy for about a day and a half and then I'd snap out of it. I'd be sitting there just feeling like nothing, and then all of a sudden I'd realize, 'Oh my, that carpet looks dirty,' and I'd want to get up and fix things and realize 'I guess I'm okay now.'"

Initially, Brown didn't want to tell people at work about her cancer. Who knows why? Perhaps she was in denial or maybe she just wanted to fight it on her own. Certainly she recalls that even as a perpetual helper, she didn't think she had the strength to help others deal with their inevitable reaction to her illness. It was enough to take care of herself.

"How was I going to help other people deal with my cancer when it was taking all of my strength to handle it myself?"

As her fortitude grew, though, she found it made her feel better to reach out to people who were also ill. Lessening the pain of others lessened her own.

"For a salesperson or someone dealing with the public, it's very easy to get really tired of people and their problems," she says. But being seriously ill changed her priorities and made her keenly sensitive to the unseen challenges others were facing. "They could be dealing with anything. Who knows what the person on the other side of the counter is coping with? They don't know what I've been through. But who am I to presume what they've been through?"

Lessening the pain of others may lessen your own.

Brown found herself less "nice" but more deeply aware and more compassionate. Since any day could be her last, she wanted to be proud of how she lived it. Impending death is a reality drug: it heightens your senses.

"Everything that's happening is a bonus. It's hard to live that, with that sort of presence, in this moment, all the time. You're here. You're alive. You have the privilege of being here."

Always a pleasant sales assistant, Brown became utterly un-flappable after her diagnosis. Customers trying to return gloves to Eaton's in downtown Toronto were in for a surprise. Wrong colour, changed your mind? No problem! Replacement? Immediately! Refund? Here you go!

"I was probably a little unbearable. I'd say, 'It's fine, we'll work on it. They're only gloves. We'll get you new ones. But isn't it a lovely day out? Call me any name in the book! I'm here! I'm alive!'"

One customer stood out. Tiny and Chinese, she'd show up every week, run her fingers gently over the gloves, smell the leather, never buy anything. "I thought, 'Well, another lonely person hanging out and that's fine.' At first, you feel badly for them."

But then Brown wondered about this stranger. Was she from out of town? Was she waiting for something? Someone? Was she alone? Yes, as it turned out, alone in Toronto and fighting cancer around the corner at St. Michael's Hospital. Her family was back in China; she was scared and dejected.

So Brown talked, shared her insights, pointed out the lessons that could be learned from battling cancer. And she encouraged her customer to fight for life, if only for the sake of her young daughter. The two women, facing the same life crisis, bonded and found themselves "fitting like a glove," Brown says, the metaphor unintended.

After that, other patients dropping by the accessories department would have their spirits lifted by Brown, as did eventually some doctors. They bought gloves, they bought scarves, and they went away with Brown's message in their hearts. "Live! Every day is precious!"

Brown's family was adamant they should try everything conceivable to prolong her life, including a costly radiation therapy available only in the United States. Magically, or so it seemed to Brown, a long-forgotten share of her father's estate was discovered and cashed to subsidize her trip.

In 1998, she travelled to New York City and stayed in a Staten Island apartment owned by the hospital. She underwent seven weeks of radiation therapy, focused not on her bowel cancer, but on the tumours in her liver. As best she could, Brown treated the whole thing like a holiday, sharing her little flat with her many Canadian visitors, shopping and strolling through art galleries between treatments. So popular did "Brown's Cancer Adventure" become, she eventually had to turn away would-be visitors.

"Perhaps it's a terrible thing to say to people in the sense that I was there for treatment, but I had a great time. I was in Manhattan every other day, friends came, we went to museums and I felt good."

For anyone who has cancer or has watched another suffer with it, there are no surefire "cures." But Brown's earlier tragedies had forced an emotional evolution in her that paid off when she received her diagnosis. Accustomed to doing what she was told, stifling her own concerns and counting on others to protect her, she would likely have been a very different patient had it not been for her earlier marital crisis and personal losses. From that chaos emerged a feisty, determined Brown who trusted herself above all others.

Not only did she insist on knowing everything about her condition and its treatment, she reached beyond the scientific world of Western medicine into alternative therapies. Improved nutrition—the elimination of high-fat junk food, her favourite chocolate, caffeine, red meat and alcohol—gave her body a fighting chance. But she didn't stop there. Her desire to learn how to meditate and harness the emotional and intellectual power of the mind to heal the body led her to some of the most spiritual people in Canada. In the autumn of 1996, she stepped into the tranquil home office of Toronto's Dr. Allistair Cunningham, himself a cancer survivor, and learned how to visualize and meditate.

Some medical experts believe our bodies heal best when in their most calm and restful state, yet the medical procedures that often accompany illness push us to the opposite end of the stress spectrum. Brown found the long periods in the hospital waiting rooms to be especially frightening.

"Someone on the other side of the office wall is going to tell you whether you live or die. But they're having lunch or talking about last night's movie. I know they have to have a life, but my life is in their hands and I have to sit here and wait and try to read a magazine. I cannot even look at it," she recalls.

———————

A year later, Brown joined a unique cancer patients' support organization called Wellspring, in Toronto. So far she hasn't left, although now she's doing the helping.

Wellspring is located in a pretty white house in the centre of Toronto's vibrant gay village. Inside, it looks like a tony residence, soft and plush and quiet. There, Brown practised meditating, visualizing her cancer so she could send it healing thoughts.

"You are actually encouraged to know where the cancer is in your body and bring the power of your mind to counteract it, and to make your body stronger and healthier," she says.

"When I learned to meditate I could get that power back that I lost in the waiting room. I'd know I was going to be fine and it wasn't just up to the medical staff.

"You do the best you can do to save me. I'll do the best I can do. But it's not your responsibility whether I live or not. You tell me what you know and I'll take that, but I do not have to sit here and wait because it's going to be what it's going to be."

With practice, Brown was eventually able to meditate for long periods, something she insisted upon doing before each visit to the doctor or hospital because it helped make the waiting-room time less stressful. In that calm state, she took back the personal control she'd relinquished during the shock of her first diagnosis. She was able to unravel much of her anxiety, and find answers that had previously eluded her.

Most importantly, Brown says, she regained her ability to hope. That's a scarce commodity when you're carrying around a six-month termination notice. She remembers the uplifting words of the American surgeon and author Bernie Siegel, who has been known to issue a challenge to physicians with terminal patients: Are they willing to bet a year of their salary that a patient will die within the deadline they've predicted? "If they cannot bet their wages, there is hope," Brown says.

When she meditates—sitting in a quiet room, eyes closed, mind cleared of thought—Brown visits the land of hope where no diagnosis is certain, and every death sentence open to appeal.

"You're telling me that I'm not going to live, but there is a voice in the back of my mind that says, 'I may live longer than you. You don't know that. You could be out the door today with a brain aneurysm.'

"Who knows? I understand that cancer is serious and that this may happen and that's fine because I need that information, but I also need you to have that door a little bit open to hope. I need the experts to say, 'Mary, it's not looking good but we'll do the best we can.'"

It was also in her meditation that Mary explored her own true feelings about dying. "I asked, 'Am I going to live?' The answer that popped right back was: 'Live as though you are going to live.' We do that anyway. None of us knows whether we are going to live another ten minutes."

Think about it: Do *you* have ten minutes more? Who really knows?

"Look at all those poor people on 9/11. The fear that people have had since the terrorist attack is very similar to the fear that people with cancer have. Life is very tenuous."

Live as though you are going to live.

But to go beyond survival and truly thrive, Brown says, you must let go of what you thought you knew about how long life would last. We never really know. Any control we believe 9/11 or cancer or an accident or tragedy took from us was never ours in the first place. While the circumstances that lead to death may be shocking, death itself is not, actually, a shock. And once we acknowledge that life's end can take any form, at any time, the shock of that can be digested, too.

"Then the anxiety of *when* you are going to die passes. You start living as though you're going to live, because what other choice is there? I do not want to live as though I am going to die because then it is already over. Live—truly live—until you die."

It has been eight years and counting since Mary Brown was diagnosed with Stage-four terminal colon cancer and given as little as six months to live. Does she know why she is alive today when so many others have succumbed? Not really.

"Maybe there is somebody up there pulling strings. It's sort of the enlightenment of your soul. Your soul is being challenged to become wise. For global wisdom perhaps. So everything that you go through—if you get through and you handle it—allows you to be that little bit wiser, that little bit more compassionate, more forgiving, that little bit more God-like."

Still, Brown admits that when faced with your own demise you wonder whether anything you do really matters. She found her answer quickly—every time she volunteered to comfort others and saw that it helped. She discovered new feelings, experienced deeper insights, and encouraged others to do the same. And she accomplished all of this while she was supposed to be saying good-bye. She uses some of that new-found time to inspire others.

She volunteers at Wellspring, taking phone calls from those in shock over their diagnosis, meeting and meditating, talking, holding hands, helping others see the bend in the road as an opportunity, rather than a final omen.

"I am really at the point where I think everything we do does matter. How we present practically every minute of the day—how we talk to anybody. It all matters.

"You think of all those little instances where you get on the bus and the bus driver is really nice to everybody and makes a joke, when everybody gets off and has a better day—it matters."

Every minute matters, Brown insists. Sick or healthy, poor or wealthy, succeeding or failing—everything *you* do, the very next thing *you* do, makes a difference.

When Brown's friend called recently, whining about her fiftieth birthday, wondering how she'd cope with aging, the new Mary was incredulous—and said so.

"Fifty! That's amazing! It's incredible you've made it to fifty! It is incredible any of us make it to *any* age. Aren't we lucky?"

MULUGETA ABAI

Torture:

1. Infliction of severe bodily pain, e.g.,
as punishment or means of persuasion

2. Subject to torture (tortured to extract a confession;
tortured with neuralgia or anxiety; (fig.) force
out of natural position or state...

MULUGETA ABAI does not want your pity. For two decades, in fact, he told no one about his life. The usual inducements to conversation, especially about the past, are useless. He has swung from the dank, dripping ceilings of Ethiopia's palace of torture, wrists twisted and handcuffed beneath his legs. He knows your tricks.

Any question is a threat. A simple inquiry a prelude to arrest. He does not make small talk because talk, he has discovered, is always big.

To look at, Abai is a plain man, slight with dark grey hair. You probably wouldn't notice him on the street; but then, that's his plan. He distorts himself to disappear—shoulders narrowed and inhaled, head neither erect nor bowed, cloaked in anonymity.

Every day, he drives carefully to his job in downtown Toronto, where he started in a junior position and worked his way up to director. He is firm. He is efficient. He is distant.

There are clues, though, about Abai's Ethiopian past. One of them is the job he has chosen for himself in his adopted country: he runs the Canadian Centre for Victims of Torture.

Clients say he offers them comfort, that he is perceptive, kind, and always determined to help them. But they never get the truth: that behind his murmurs of understanding there is his own vivid recall, and that behind his sympathy there are the shifting sheets he returns to each night, tossing in nightmares he refuses to share with his wife, who lies awake, wondering.

It is difficult to interview a torture victim about torture. The structural parallels are too acute.

Interview = interrogation.

Inquiry = inquisition.

A journalist may retreat, but a torturer never does. More than two decades later, Abai wants to believe he can now tell the difference. He has invited a journalist into his home and he wants to talk. He braces himself nevertheless.

He explains that this is because people who've been tortured—bitten and mauled by animals or beaten, raped, and cut by human beings—afterward have a difficult time distinguishing a polite inquiry from intense interrogation, a traffic ticket from a harbinger of death.

"They have very low self-esteem," Abai says. "They are afraid of authority, so even though they know, for example, that the Canadian police are different from the police back home, what they see when they are stopped for a traffic ticket is not the image of the Canadian police. What they see is the soldier who has brutalized them, humiliated them."

Abai can remember a peaceful, predictable life before his imprisonment at the hands of a dictator. He was born in 1953 in the northern Ethiopian province of Tigray, the first of seven children, with plenty to eat and nice clothes to wear. His father, a lower-court judge educated in France and Italy, sent his sons to boarding school during the week and impressed upon them the importance of education. They played, too. Abai remembers running and jumping and sunshine and fun.

Later, when university recruiters suggested Abai try a career in teaching, it fit: "Teaching is like nurturing a plant. You see the children grow."

Abai married at twenty-one, and would have four sons. Eventually he was promoted from school principal to district educational director, overseeing some sixty elementary and secondary schools in the province of Gondar. Studious, committed, loyal, Abai says he took his work and his family seriously. But this quietly rewarding life was unfolding against a backdrop of political upheaval that would eventually envelop and destroy it.

In 1974, the Ethiopian emperor Haile Selassie was overthrown by the Dergue, a leftist populist movement led by the military, and initially supported by Abai and other intellectuals. Under the slogan of "bloodless revolution" the new leaders promised a more democratic society, with land redistribution and a socialist approach to community services. But brutal political in-fighting and the rise of ruthless Mengistu Haile Mariam transformed the Dergue from liberators to executioners. Mengistu, deranged and power-hungry, began to terrorize the very people who'd supported him during the revolution.

In 1976, Abai was transferred to a neighbouring school district. His family was not invited to accompany him, so Abai took the bus alone, suitcase in hand, and checked into a hotel. He realized his mistake immediately.

In the lobby, on the stairs, in the dining room, there were grim-faced "government cadres" and soldiers. The hotel was full of supporters of Mengistu, the man who'd slaughtered his military rivals and would soon launch mass executions known as the "Red Terror." His main targets were the young and the academics. People like Mulugeta Abai.

By now, it was widely known that Dergue soldiers were killing civilians without evidence, let alone trials. "They would simply detain people, take them out and shoot them and leave them on the street for days. It was very shocking," Abai says.

Afraid he would arouse suspicion if he quickly checked out of the hotel, and hours away from friends and family, Abai stayed, nodding politely as the soldiers passed him each morning on the way to breakfast.

On the ninth day, he and two officials from the ministries of agriculture and health were arrested by Mengistu's men. "These are the social cadres, specifically trained to agitate people, to look for reactionaries, to spread the gospel of socialism. My job was to educate the children, to produce the future labour force for the country, to work with teachers. I was a target," he says.

In jail, the three detainees, who might otherwise have supported each other, huddled alone and ate in silence, terrified that one among them might be a Mengistu informant, planted there to spy on the others.

Eventually, the three men discovered they were suspected of being supporters of the opposition. Abai was accused of allowing traitors to use education ministry typewriters and photocopiers to dispatch anti-Mengistu flyers. And although Abai would eventually begin to work actively with fellow academics to oust Mengistu, he says he was not doing so at the time of his arrest. In

fact, looking back, Abai says the repeated bouts of false imprisonment are what spawned his eventual rebellion. "When you are not
actively involved but you are considered to be actively involved,
it is better to be actively involved and then accept the consequences. That's what the Dergue were doing: pushing people to
oppose them and not to work peacefully."

On the ninth day of his imprisonment, Abai's cellmates were
shaken awake, walked outside and executed. Their bodies were
tossed into the street, their blood streaming from bullet wounds.
"They were not even interrogated," he whispers.

Abai was released. He suspects that he was spared because
authorities eventually realized he was a stranger in their area
without friends or contacts. He returned to the same hotel that
housed the Dergue, stiffly feigning a fearlessness he hoped would
suggest he had nothing to hide. Going home wasn't an option; if
he failed to show up to do his job it would be seen as disobedi-
ence or a show of independence, which would inevitably cause
trouble for his young family and make them targets, as well.
Besides, special passes, available only from a government agency,
were required to travel from one municipality to another.

Abai's relief was short-lived. Some six months later he attended
an educational conference of school supervisors and district educational officers in the provincial capital. One morning, as he
stopped in the street to have his shoes polished, a driver roared to
a stop and warned him Mengistu's soldiers were once again after
him. They'd already rounded up seventeen of his colleagues and
two students. Abai tried to leave quietly through the back door of
his hotel, but came face to face with four gunmen.

"I knew if I moved they would kill me, because they were told
that I was armed and dangerous. But I've never operated a gun!"
He points to his chest where they'd pressed the barrels of their
weapons, and recalls how they barked at him. "So I followed."

Shocked passersby watched as the small man with the bent
head and shaking hands was pushed through the streets.

This time, Abai was taken directly to an old palace, once a king's retreat, now a chamber of horrors. He'd seen men return from this makeshift dungeon with their feet awash in their own blood.

As a high-ranking education official in the midst of student uprisings, he was accused, once again, of being a ringleader. In the middle of the night they called his name twice, and he believed that it was his turn to die. He felt nothing but the numbness that follows terror.

A surprise awaited him outside, though: not a firing squad, but the deputy governor of the district in which Abai lived and worked. Apparently, he hadn't appreciated learning that his Dergue colleagues from the city of Gondar had ransacked his territory for fresh prisoners. The military official arranged to have the prisoners, including Abai, transported back to his own district, where they remained in jail for more than four months. A game of political one-upmanship had saved Abai's life—for now.

"A lot of people were being detained. A lot of people were being executed. I think we were the lucky ones, even to stay alive," he says.

For the first few weeks of his imprisonment the routine was strict: twenty minutes in the morning and the afternoon, no more, to wash and use the toilet. Later, the political prisoners, who were held without explanation or charge, were put to work tending the gardens around the prison compound, and permitted only occasional visits from relatives.

Abai can still see and smell it all with tremendous clarity—the bulky outline of the prison, the winding irrigation system they cobbled together for the plants, the dull desperation, the glorious, pitiful sense of accomplishment at having lived one more day. "It's not something that goes away."

But where did he put the anger, the frustration, the sense of injustice most people in the Western world now express so readily?

"I had those feelings, but you cannot articulate them. You will end up dead. So, you have to keep all that to yourself. You couldn't even trust your friends or your co-workers, because some of them could be plants."

Shock gives way to anger. Anger, pent up, erodes the soul. Captivity eats ambition. "You age very quickly. It's hopelessness, really. That's what it creates."

Ironically, imprisonment failed as a deterrent to would-be challengers of Mengistu's dictatorship; instead, it hardened Ethiopians' desire for change. The endless torture only underscored the importance of the protestors' demand for rights and freedoms. Thinking back, Abai says, "I would probably have felt guilty if I had not been involved. A lot of my friends and colleagues were killed for talking about democratic rights."

So, when Abai was released from prison a second time, again under arbitrary circumstances but this time "pardoned," he and his colleagues adopted new tactics. Rather than openly question Mengistu, they infiltrated his organization. They gathered intelligence and used it to warn those whom Mengistu and his cronies were targeting for detention or death. They managed to get "a lot of people" out of prison, too. But the silent underground never plotted violent rebellion, he insists. Mengistu and the Dergue were too powerful.

By this time, however, Abai was among "the previously detained," the usual suspects who were arrested repeatedly as men broke under the torture and spat out names, to curry favour or still an inquisitor's hand. And so it was that one day, as he was attending a literacy program, soldiers burst into the auditorium shouting his name, dragged him out of the building and shoved him into a Land Rover.

For more than twenty years, what happened next remained Abai's secret, one he refused to share with his ex-wife or children, even though it meant they might never understand or forgive him.

On an early autumn afternoon in Canada, Abai decides he wants to explain, not to someone close, but to a stranger. Her shock and sorrow will not injure him as much as the tears of his new Canadian wife, who would certainly weep to hear what was done to her beloved husband in a country so far away.

He wants to talk because he has come to understand that releasing memory into the light can dry up its poison. But he also shares his story as a testament to what the human spirit can endure; perhaps it will reach someone else who is suffering and offer some hope.

Abai hesitates at first, but once he begins to speak of the past, he will not stop, cannot stop. With each sentence, his face contorts and he cries. Yet slowly, his hunched shoulders straighten and widen, imperceptibly at first and then forcefully. He is sitting up, staring back, relieved and emboldened by speaking the truth. He has decided to talk, on his own terms, and he will say later that he knows he made a wise decision. Because he can no longer hide from his family; the price he paid has already been too steep. Because some day his four sons may understand why he had to leave them.

Hearing what others survived
gives us faith it can be done.

The Ethiopian jail cells to which Abai is dragged are small, fetid and crammed with prisoners, many starving and delirious. The political prisoners are held in a "prison within a prison." The floors are filthy, caked with layers of insects and human excrement. With as many as sixty people in one cell, many must take turns lying on the ground to rest. The exhausted or ill, too weak to wait their turn for a space on the floor, close their eyes and pass out standing up.

Locked in. Terror-stricken. No newspapers, no radios. Nothing but buckets for toilets inside the cells. Anyone who falls ill in the middle of the night is left suffering. Perhaps a guard, after finishing his morning coffee, will amble off to find a doctor.

One surreal evening, Abai listens as, one by one, the names of almost fifty of the prisoners surrounding him are shouted out and one by one they are led away. There is no sleep as the roll call of death drones on—university students, teachers and medical doctors escorted to slaughter. In the morning, there are only six men left. The silence is so deep that the buzz of a single fly is deafening to Abai.

"They took them and killed them, all of them. Some of them were very innocent. Very, very innocent," Abai says, his voice, even today, quavering in disbelief.

Shot, the bodies hidden, nothing left but their clothes, to be handed over when relatives came calling on Sunday.

The sadness is overwhelming. "That your government did it to you. A government that's supposed to look after its own people. The future generations who could have probably helped the country move from poverty. Children who have grown up without parents. Wives who have aged without their husbands. Mothers who are still crying, wondering where their children are." These are the thoughts that churn through the prisoner's mind, that haunt him still.

But in the cell Abai and his fellow survivors cannot cry, dare not make a sound. They wait for another two days, unable to sleep, dreading their own end. Mute, they watch as another wave of prisoners is corralled to replace those now dead. Powerlessness pummels Abai; physical torture is soon added to the emotional terrorism of murder and silent mourning.

Doors slam. Abai! Abai! His name is being called. "You know that you are going to be interrogated," Abai says. "You know that you are going to be tortured. They take you from the prison. They take you to the torture chambers."

There is, first, the horror of hearing friends die and the torment of being unable to help them. Then there is physical pain— the soul-piercing agony of being twisted and beaten.

Today, dressed in neatly pressed pants and a short-sleeved cotton shirt, Abai lifts his arms to expose the rubbery ridge of a scar on his wrist: that's where they tightened the handcuffs until they broke his flesh and his blood squirted up like a fountain.

Handcuffs are clasped around his wrists and a metal pole thrust through his locked hands and feet, so he's forced to curl in a fetal position

Two men, muscled and mean, hoist the pole and suspend Abai from the ceiling, spinning him like a trussed turkey on a barbecue spit. "Every time you swing as they are hitting you, the handcuffs tighten up," he says.

The soldiers take turns lashing the soles of Abai's feet with leather whips, while a third yells and screams, demanding the names of his co-conspirators. Time dissolves. "It's very difficult to tell how long it lasts, even if it is two or three minutes, it is a very long time."

For Abai, a teacher who has poured his life's energy into educating young people, there is an even greater horror: the third torturer is one of his former students, someone he knows well. "He pretended to be the good guy. It was brutal. I taught him in grades seven and eight. That's a betrayal."

This ravaging of civil society torments Abai, too. His pupil was one of many "who are picked up from the streets, who didn't have anything. I think his father died, and now they have all the power and all the money. It's this type of people who are dangerous."

Yet, having looked into the bare face of cruelty, Abai says he never lost his belief in human goodness. "But you lose the trust. It becomes very difficult to establish some sort of relationship. You become very suspicious."

For twenty-two months, Abai was held in jail, tortured and traumatized. Each day he awoke knowing it could be his last. At one

point, called for yet another session of beatings, he grew convinced he would be killed. He slipped his wedding ring from his
finger and urged his fellow prisoners to return it to his wife—if
anyone got out of the prison alive.

Then, inexplicably, Abai was released. His old job was gone,
but he was moved to another district near the national capital of
Addis Ababa and demoted to school principal. Once again, relief
would not last long. The following year, he was tipped off that
Mengistu's men were again looking for him, on the way to search
his parents' home. He knew he couldn't take the chance of being
captured again. So he bolted in the middle of the night, leaving
behind his parents, his wife and his four sons. He left to protect
them. "I believed I had no choice," he says.

It was a decision that would forever alter the course of many
lives.

It took Mulugeta Abai, educator and father, seventeen days
of walking and hitchhiking through the dark night and hiding in
churches or in the brush during the day to reach the Sudanese
border. "I was terrified that I would be caught. I had experienced
three detentions, so the fourth time would not be easy."

The fourth time would almost certainly be deadly.

"I had only one shirt and one sweater and a small cloth that
I used as a blanket and it was dirty. I was dirty. So I don't think
people would recognize me," he says of his journey toward freedom. He still has that shirt.

Although Abai did not speak Arabic, he quickly found a job
teaching English in refugee camp schools run by the Sudan
Council of Churches, a missionary group funded by the Swedish
government. In 1982, the International Catholic Migration Com-
mission hired him to teach people who were preparing to reset-
tle in the United States.

Certain he would be imprisoned if he returned to Ethiopia,
Abai was eventually granted asylum in Australia and Canada. He
arrived in Vancouver in 1983. He was equally certain that his

family would be imprisoned and tortured if authorities had any clue of his whereabouts. So Abai did not contact his wife or four children, although he knew he risked losing their love. It was his love for them, though, that kept him going, and made him put as much distance as possible between himself and them.

Although Abai went back to visit his Ethiopian family in 1991, the year Mengistu was ousted, and again in 1996, the couple eventually divorced. He never tried to justify himself. "She's entitled to be angry, because I left her there with four kids to raise by herself," he says of his first wife.

On his own in a safer but strange country, Abai was focused on nothing more than survival. Unable to find a job on the West Coast, he moved to Toronto. He went to work in an airplane parts factory and spent his free time studying political science at York University.

Yet despite his loneliness and the ever-present paranoia of the tortured, Abai says he never considered giving up.

"The will to live and my children kept me going. I have to be strong, and for my friends who passed, who were executed, I didn't want to give in."

Of a dozen close friends, only he and one other, now living in the United States, made it out of Ethiopia alive.

"Every time I remember my friends, every time I see their children, I feel guilty for surviving when others have perished." He has spent many years since trying to make sense of those odds.

It is that conundrum, perhaps, that underlies Abai's spiritual transformation. Although he was raised in the Ethiopian Orthodox Church, he'd never embraced Christianity in a meaningful way until he was imprisoned. It was behind bars that he found faith.

"I think I survived because somebody higher up protected me. I could easily have given the names of my associates and friends. I could easily have destroyed a lot of families. I was able to keep that information intact and to save a lot of lives; I don't think I did it by myself. Somebody else somewhere was helping me keep that information and be strong."

He rejects the possibility that he simply may have been much more resilient, both physically and psychologically, than he ever realized. "No, it was beyond anything I could have done. It was God." Rather than blame God for his torture, he credits him with his salvation.

Abai remarried in 1994 and now he and his new wife have two daughters. He has already brought two of his sons to Canada from Ethiopia, and helped them complete university. He dreams of reuniting his entire family.

Talking about what happened to him inside those prison walls is an important first step to healing and perhaps ending those nightmares, he says. He knows he must relearn the joy of communication. He must find his way back to trust. Like the torture victims he helps every day, Abai says he must accept that confidences do not always lead to confinement. Questions can be posed out of concern. Answers can lead to assistance, understanding and greater love.

And now, every day on the job, Abai works to give that knowledge to other torture victims. He delivers that information, of course, in words of assurance. But he has also devoted himself to repairing the damage by replacing bad experience with good. When victims come to him, he listens. He allows them to talk—or not. He allows them to stay with him—or not. He provides choices and tries to encourage the confidence to make them. He works to restore what was taken from them, but is careful to take nothing more, to ask for nothing more than they appear able to give.

"I encourage people to take the steps that they are comfortable with to start the healing process. One has to be ready to talk about one's own experiences and seek professional help if needed."

Help is only help if you are ready to receive it.

But always, Abai teaches those who have survived to respect themselves for having done so—and to honour their own emotional compass as they set out in their new lives.

"They are agents of their own recovery. It is okay not to talk if one is not ready to do so."

Put yourself in charge of your own recovery.

As the executive director of the Canadian Centre for Victims of Torture, Abai is responsible not only for running the place, but for pushing public education and policy development. He is teaching an end to torture.

The centre, funded by government at all levels as well as the United Nations, the United Way and grassroots groups, assists survivors of torture in their transition from terrorized victims to healthy, involved community members. Abai and his colleagues arrange counselling, crisis intervention, individual and group therapy, help with language and legal problems, even computer instruction. "Volunteer friends"—people who understand the insidious effect of torture—are also found to help victims adjust to life after terror.

It is not simply a matter of offering comfort, Abai says.

So often, victims turn on themselves after being abused, blaming themselves and feeling humiliated, even though it was others who behaved inhumanly toward them. It is a thought process Abai understands far too well. It happened to him.

Intellectually, he says, he knows he is not to blame. He readily agrees that he and other torture victims did nothing wrong. He says he understands that the crimes perpetrated were not their fault; if anything, victims deserve respect for having the strength to survive.

But in a jail cell, when you are stripped of basic human freedom amid the wails of dying friends, the mind convulses and the heart breaks.

"You are treated like an animal, caged like an animal. It's a very bad experience to see your children cry. I remember one Sunday when they came to visit me; my son was about three years old the last time I was detained. There was a fence, and the visitors were far away. He just crushed the fence and came to me. I couldn't even lift him. He just burst into tears. And he wouldn't let me go either.

"What's more humiliating than not being able to be there when your children need you? It's a betrayal, even though I had no choice."

He missed much of his sons' childhood because he was imprisoned or running from torture. But he will grant himself no leniency.

Doesn't he think his children, once they know of his ordeal, will understand that he had no choice and be proud of his bravery?

"They might be also angry as well, you know. At me, for not being there when they were growing up."

Would that be right? "Oh, yes," he says, quickly.

But wouldn't it be unfair to blame him for an absence he could not prevent?

"I know . . . But I don't blame them. It's my responsibility. I brought them into this world. I have a responsibility to bring them up. Maybe when they are old enough we will sit down and talk about it. But they won't understand it when they are young. They will not. It's very difficult."

And, so, Mulugeta Abai is still the teacher he set out to be before evil intervened. Free in Canada, why does he not go back to the sweet scent of chalk and the succour of routine? Why spend his weekdays reliving the experience of others' torture, and his weekends recovering?

"At times it brings back those painful memories, but it has also given me an excellent opportunity to heal. It would have been very difficult for me to deal with my personal experiences had I been working in any other area. I think I can easily relate to those who come seeking our services and can assist in the creation of a conducive atmosphere where the healing process can take place."

In the end, Abai's torture is also his calling.

"You have to see the positive side as well. Why does one survive while others perish? We were fifty-four in a room, only six or seven of us were left. We didn't have any power to say that no, we are not going to go there."

And that has left Abai with a profound sense of responsibility. "Yes! I should work very hard to prevent such things from happening. I should work very hard also to help people who have had similar experiences move from that victim environment and be productive citizens. That is a commitment I have."

Your crisis may be your calling.

Abai smiles, not very often, but it comes. "It's very rewarding. When you try to help people who have gone through similar experiences, and when you see them change over time, that's very rewarding."

Yet this teacher, this restorer of souls and keeper of faith has a long journey ahead of him still. After he finally revealed to his wife and two of his four sons a few details of his past trauma, there was some relief. "I think they were shocked when they first learned about my past. They were also upset that I had to live with the pain for a long time."

Each person with whom we share our past has the potential to join our circle of support. "A network of trusted friends could be the key to overcoming the pain. Studies done on Holocaust survivors show that community support is key to gaining one's self-esteem and overcoming traumatic experiences.

"I get the courage to continue from the love and responsibility I have towards my children. I also draw courage from the many people who have gone through horrible experiences and come to the Canadian Centre for Victims of Torture. I admire their resiliency and will to live."

Now, he is committed to being there for his two young daughters. And some day, he hopes, all of his sons will understand that the pain of his torture pales in comparison to his missing their youth.

"I hope they will understand. Time will tell."

DOUG DANE

---

*A young boy adopted by abusive, alcoholic
parents and lured into a ring of pedophiles
transcends his shame to rescue others.*

THERE ARE NO PHOTOGRAPHS, no teething rings, no fuzzy stuffed animals—no treasured mementos of any kind—from the first six months of Doug Dane's life. There is nothing but a single paragraph written in a hurried hand and buried in a Children's Aid Society report.

It describes the foundling's fleeting stay with a foster family somewhere in Ontario. The names of the town and the family are both now meaningless to him. The gist of the brief note is that the infant boy, Dane, didn't cry much. He would spend a lifetime making up for that.

Today, Dane believes he is the fifth of six children born to his mother and four different fathers. The woman refuses to admit she gave birth to Dane, although detective work suggests that she did, in 1963. And years later, Dane still does not know the identity of his biological father.

What little Dane does know of his origins, and of the circumstances that set him on such a haphazard course in life, he gleaned from the interviews he conducted later, as an adult, after he became determined to build himself a past.

And then there are the few memories Dane has of his own.

———————————

Memory.

The living room of the home in which he lives with his adopted older brother and his adoptive mother and father. He is eight. His mother is drunk, ordering the boys to "Pick up the pace." It will take a week of running home from school at lunchtime and working feverishly, but they will eventually manage to repaint the entire room. It takes several coats of paint, because the bloodstains from their parents' fight are fresh and the beer spills from their mother's glass wide and wet.

Memory.

The bang, bang, bang of a hammer and a whirling drill in the basement. His father, an arthritic and alcoholic veteran of the Second World War, is installing a lock on the door of the room in which he will hide with the two boys when his wife, drunk and violent, comes swinging at them.

Memory.

You stick the tobacco into a little hole in this machine and then you put the cigarette tube on the end and you crank it around and then you throw the finished cigarette onto the pile of the other ones you've already done and then, quick! you grab more tobacco and don't you dare slow down or she'll rant and rave and hit you hard on the head.

———————————

Doug Dane was adopted in 1964. It was not the worst thing that happened to him, but nearly. Although his adoptive parents were both alcoholics—something most of their friends and family apparently knew—they had no trouble adopting not one, but two baby boys.

Why two ravaged and raging souls decided to drag children into their bleak existence, Dane says, he will never know. But he and his older brother had no choice but to stay.

A typical childhood day for Doug Dane began around seven o'clock in the morning when his mother regained consciousness in the living room of their small bungalow. They rarely had company, perhaps because the main room, where she slept, was curtainless and cluttered, piled with overflowing boxes and unsorted junk.

She kept to her schedule like clockwork. Upon waking, she immediately demanded her special concoction of beer, tomato juice and salt, and consumed it in copious amounts. The boys were expert bartenders at an early age. She was drunk by noon, when Doug was expected home from school to do his chores. Tired and lonely, Doug once dared to remain at school, eating with the other kids. Within minutes, his mother was in the schoolyard, drunk and shouting, dragging him home to work. He never tried that again.

By the time Doug was nine, his father had stopped drinking, but not before he had done his own damage. Drunk and violent most days, he beat his wife in front of the boys, threatened to blow her brains out with a shotgun and taunted her with his philandering. He gave up his Red Cap ale only after being charged with assaulting her, and he was ordered to avoid his family for a short while. His wife was in the hospital undergoing shock therapy following her third nervous breakdown, so the boys spent two peaceful months in a foster home on an Elmira farm. It would be a brief reprieve.

Later, after the unhappy group was reunited, Doug's father, now sober, took a stab at parenting. Every night, he'd take the boys out to eat. They usually had fast food, but sometimes it was a sit-down meal in a restaurant. The only home-cooked meals the boys ate were at the neighbour's house.

Then, if things were going well, they'd play sports. Soccer in the summer, or hockey in the winter. Afterward their father would take them back and they'd lie low in the recreation room until their mother passed out upstairs. That was a good day. "You were feeling really lucky if that's what happened in a day," Dane says now.

On a bad day he would be hit with a wooden spoon or a belt buckle. Sometimes their mother just used her fists to enforce her rules.

They were only permitted to tear off three squares of toilet paper when they went to the bathroom. But now and then, boys being boys, they'd slip up, or need more, or—what the hell—deliberately tear off four squares. She'd always come in to check and if they'd exceeded her quota, look out. "I can still think of the stinging feeling you get when you get hit in the face or the back of the head."

Actually, Dane can remember being struck in many different ways: punched, beaten, strapped with a belt, pummelled, smacked, pushed, clawed, squeezed, pinched, twisted, smashed. Violence was such a prominent theme in Dane's life it infiltrated his earliest speech.

His mother and aunt loved to tell the story of little Dougie, just two years old, running circles in his crib, crying out, "Strap, strap, strap, strap, strap!"

Dane remembers the two women telling that story again and again, slapping each other and laughing so hard they couldn't breathe. "It wasn't until years later, when I was grown up, that I realized that it wasn't a funny story."

When he was just twelve, Doug came home from school and found his mother, staggering drunk, swinging at his father, who was trying to renovate the basement, one of the few rooms in which the boys found refuge from her.

"I just snapped. I went nuts. The guy was just trying to build us a bigger, safer place and she was stealing it."

Doug grabbed his mother from behind, locked her in a full nelson, and carried her up the side stairs. He threw her into the driveway, and then called the police. The teen watched as his adoptive mother was hauled away, screaming at the top of her voice, "That son of a bitch tried to murder me!"

Red and blue neon police lights spun shadows on the neighbours' windows. Eyes shifted behind peepholes and noses poked from parted curtains. Years later, Dane would return to "interview" the people on that street. "They told me they'd often see us two boys hiding in the spruce bushes in front of the house. They didn't know what to do."

Life might have improved after his mother moved out, but by this time, Dane was trapped in a trajectory of tragedy.

A boy without parents, a boy without a past, he was easy pickings for those who stalk the vulnerable. It didn't take long for a predator to emerge.

Most days, Dane, thirteen, and a friend hung out at a local stereo store where the manager offered up free stereo parts and, one day, invited them to a party. "He said there would be a hundred people and good-looking girls and beer."

When the two teenagers arrived, though, the man's wife left and he wanted sex. Dane and his friend never thought to ask why the married stereo store manager, an adult twice their age, was after young boys. Strongly attracted to women, Dane resisted. But pushed by his friend, and with nowhere to go, he eventually relented.

Over the next two years, he and his friends became the playthings of a group of pedophiles, who lured more than twenty boys into homosexual sex with alcohol and the most tantalizing bait of all for lonely boys—friendship. They showed them passages in the sex manual, *The Joy of Sex*, which suggested same-sex experimenting was normal, especially in adolescence. Then they kept the boys silent by threatening to expose them to family and friends.

More than anything, Dane hated the anal sex, which "hurt and felt dirty and awful and wrong." But he was a wretched soul, who already felt unworthy and powerless.

"I hated my parents for what they were and what I'd been through. I was looking for love. These guys took care of us. They paid attention to us; they gave us stuff. They picked me up from school and we'd do things and so I was getting what I was looking for from my mom and dad."

Dane was passed from pedophile to pedophile, who took turns having sex with him and other young men.

The end of that part of his life came suddenly, and as far as Doug Dane could figure, quite by accident. One of the "usual" pedophiles and a new male friend had promised the kids a road trip to Disneyland and a kitty of $5,000 to blow. Dane left his father a note saying he wouldn't be back for a while. Dane's usual abuser showed up in a little Honda, and when the trio was well past Toronto, the perpetrator announced he was actually taking them all to Halifax, Nova Scotia. And, by the way, there really wasn't any cash, just $100 for gas. They had been kidnapped.

All the boys had to eat along the way was white bread and raw wieners. "So he tricked us. I guess he wanted to have us alone for a long time."

For a week, the three of them stayed at a borrowed Halifax apartment until, one day, Dane heard his name on the radio. The police were after them! No one had ever cared much about Dane, so he wasn't sure how to take the news. Was he a kidnap victim? Or was he in trouble for running away? He really had no idea what he was doing any more. Besides, what difference did it make?

The pedophile—worried, perhaps, about criminal charges—

took the boys back and dropped them at home. Dane's father greeted him angrily at the door, told him he was grounded for a night, and never spoke of it again.

But it wasn't over. A group of men was arrested in a flurry of headlines and scandal. Police detectives showed up at Dane's house. They had the names of boys who'd been lured into the sex ring, and they wanted more. They especially wanted details of the sexual abuse. But they left without talking to Dane's father.

When they were gone, Dane sat humiliated and scared in his basement. No one came to speak to him or comfort him. "That's probably one of the most painful things that happened to me—that my brother and my dad didn't do anything. They didn't ask. They didn't help. Nothing."

The adults' silence became the child's prison. If his father and the police didn't reach out to help him, if no adult arranged therapy or compensation, what is a boy to think?

Years later, Dane's adoptive brother would admit he'd sensed something dramatic and wrong had happened to Doug, but it never occurred to him anything could be done about it. He'd been raised, like his brother, in an environment where abuse was commonplace, and compassion unfamiliar.

Four men were later tried and convicted of sexual assault. Dane went to court but was not called to testify, which was both good and bad. "I never told my story. I never straightened out what happened to me. And I never had a conversation with my dad in my life about it, while it was happening or as I grew older."

By fifteen, Dane had endured—and survived—two years of sexual abuse and a lifetime of destructive parents. His mother lived at the YWCA after she left the family; sometimes he'd see her on the street and cross to the other side to avoid her. His father, cowering and absent, became even more debilitated. "I think as I became a teenager, I was the parent," he says.

Unfortunately, he began to imitate his parents far too closely. For the next dozen years, he was drunk or stoned on drugs constantly. He stopped and started high school three times and, today, has about the equivalent of a grade nine education.

He married twice, first when he was twenty-eight, again at thirty-four, and divorced twice, always balking when his partners pressed for more intimacy, particularly sexual. He never told them, or anyone, what had happened to him at the hands of the pedophiles.

And he lied.

"I was never able to express myself openly and I would manipulate situations to turn things around and make it their fault. I became resentful of their families. It was odd, because I was thankful that they welcomed me, but at the same time I didn't feel I deserved it. Often I would criticize my second wife's family about how they operated, yet I had no right to question how their family rules worked."

But, then, Dane had been lying all his life. It was one of the few skills his parents had taught him. "I was threatened with punishment if I didn't lie about what was going on in our home. Mom told me I would get strapped if I told anyone."

So he lied to stay out of trouble; he lied to get attention; he lied to relieve his emotional distress.

"I remember one time when I was in grade seven, while I was being sexually abused. I was a long distance runner and I was running a race at a track meet and it was one of the few times my dad was there. I faked a major cramp and pretended to black out during the race. I carried the lie on even to the point of going to the doctors for an examination and still pretending I was ill. I was so desperate for attention and love that I had to lie to get it."

He fabricated so much of his life that he had no sense of really living at all. "I cheated on every woman I ever had a relationship with. I stole money from my father and brother. I'd made up so many stories in my life, they had become the truth for me."

To live a lie is painful, confusing,
frustrating and empty.

Are there epiphanies in our lives, or do we simply, perhaps unknowingly, reach a point where we cannot continue on the same road?

For Dane, that nadir came as his second marriage was ending. Despite earlier stints with "superficial" counselling, a broken engagement and a painful first divorce, he says that absolutely nothing had changed in him. His second marriage had been a mirror image of all his other relationships, fraught with fear of intimacy and constant anxiety that his partner would see through him to the real Doug—the ugly, shameful, dirty, evil person he believed himself to be. "It's ironic, isn't it? I was so afraid they would leave me, that I left them first," he says now.

"All along as a young boy, I swore I wouldn't become my parents. I would do anything to avoid that. I really wanted to make my marriage work. I didn't want to fail again. I was successful in other areas of my life and I felt if I can do what I set my mind to in business, I could do it in relationships."

It was that desperate determination—not to ruin yet another marriage—that launched Dane on a real path to changing his life, and cleaning up his act.

"People tell me that I have courage, but I don't think it takes guts. I think it takes a high level of *desire*. You have to be motivated to heal."

You will not heal unless you
truly want to. Period.

For Dane, that motivation came from finally seeing and accepting that he was hurting too many people, including himself. "I was living a lie. I was in the wrong places my whole life. I knew I was destined for something else."

So he went back to therapy in 2000, but this time he was determined to benefit from the process. He found a female counsellor who seemed to understand him, and he made himself do the work, to face the "voices" of hurt and pain and anger that had stalked him and hissed at him his whole life.

"People can try to help you for a thousand years, but you have to really want that help, even if you don't think you deserve it. Eventually, you realize that the fact that you need help so badly is directly related to how much you deserve help. Do the math."

The first and perhaps the most enduring change Dane made was trying to weed out the deceit in his life. "How much of what you do is a lie? I lied to myself about how I felt, about what I was accomplishing. And I assumed that lying to everyone else was necessary just to continue." He hid his past; he hid his present; now, he wanted to learn how to expose himself to the future.

Although his second marriage would prove to be beyond saving, Dane took what he considered to be a huge risk and revealed his past sexual abuse. His soon-to-be ex-wife listened quietly and then gently told him she thought there must have been something wrong; she had sensed it. "She just held me and handled it beautifully and we cried."

Even today, thinking back on the relationships he sacrificed to keep the secret of abuse, he aches. "I don't live my life with regrets any more, but certainly when I relive it, I cry."

Despite his initial success in therapy, and the warm reception his truth-telling elicited, Dane reached an impasse and stumbled around in counselling for more than a year. He'd turned over many of the stones in his past, seen the worms wriggling away and made progress toward placing the blame where it belonged: not on himself, but on those whose cruelty or carelessness had blighted his childhood and sabotaged his manhood.

But he was stuck, unable to move past his memories. He was still depressed. He doubted his abilities. He was convinced he was unlovable, damaged goods. And despite the nice talk, he believed deep down that the best way to stay "emotionally safe" was to never again risk feeling any real emotion. Especially love. Especially sexuality.

"I kept trying to reach inside to a place where I could find a sense of self, a courage, some knowledge that I was worthy of living well. I just saw a lot of darkness."

Where, he kept wondering, do you look for an emotional foundation when you were never given the chance to build one? When every relationship of trust you ever touched blew up in your face?

Yet despite his self-loathing and sense of betrayal, Dane eventually managed to spin new trust out of gossamer threads. Slowly, he came to trust one person—his therapist. She earned that trust, of course, and to this day when Dane speaks of her you can be forgiven for thinking he means his mother.

In session after session, his guide acknowledged how difficult it was for Dane to trust again. She admitted to him that trust is never a sure thing: it is a leap of faith. But all the talk means nothing if you cannot take one more chance with humanity and try to trust again, to live without constantly guarding your heart. "In order to trust," she told Dane, "you need to have faith, and the key to faith is letting go. If you let go, you can live."

> **Talk means nothing unless you take
> one more chance on humanity.**

Still, for Dane the leap seemed too big, the gulf too wide to span. He says he knew he was right there on the cliff of renewal, but he remained too scared and too hurt to jump.

One day, he cried out to his therapist: "I can't get over there. It's too far. I can't jump that far."

She looked into his eyes and said kindly, "Don't jump, Doug. Fly."

Don't jump. Fly.

And then Dane felt it: the magic of human faith. And the power, too, that comes when someone—the therapist, in his case—believes you are capable of more.

In that moment, Dane began to let go of his anger, self-doubt, recrimination and his shame. How could he fly with that cargo? More importantly, his therapist had helped him understand that his heavy load need not be transported at all.

Put down what is too heavy to carry.
You probably don't need it.

Freed of the weight of all the lies and guilt, Dane started pitching emotional garbage overboard like the captain of a sinking ship. He had been sinking, he realized, and *he* had the power to lighten his burden.

Not only did he tell many more people what had happened to him as a child, he intensified his search for more details. No longer ashamed of what had been done to him, he was keen to assemble a past, and find the good that had once existed in the little Dane boy.

He visited old family friends, neighbours and people he remembered only meeting once. He begged for their memories of him, his life and his bizarre parents. He interviewed old teachers, Children's Aid Society workers, even the detectives who'd investigated his abuse case years before. He demanded to know why so little had been done to help him. Many times the answers were frustrating, futile and painful.

Why did the authorities permit two alcoholics to adopt two children, especially when friends had mentioned the addiction?

Oh, dear, who knows, Doug, who knows?

Why didn't the detectives tell his parents about the sexual abuse and arrange some medical help for him?

That's not how things were done then, son.

Why didn't his teachers report his many injuries and investigate their source?

You hid them too well, Doug.

But when he didn't get the answers he wanted, Dane learned to live with that, too. He couldn't change his past. He accepted that. Resenting everyone and everything for the rest of his life guaranteed the rest of his life would be as lousy as the beginning.

So, he sorted. The memories of pain and exploitation he threw away. Cut the chains and hurled them like rusty anchors off his sleek new sailboat. The memories he liked—a few good times with friends; his own sense of mischief; his father's clumsy but well-intentioned attempts to protect his adopted sons—he kept.

Sort your memories; keep the good ones.

Then he turned his mind to his personal life. Fortunately for Dane, he had a flair for business. He has a good head for numbers; and his emotional detachment, born of abuse, was a real boon when negotiating. It was while working as a financial consultant that he started dating a vivacious real estate agent, Gia Lucchetta. One of the first things he told the new woman in his life, now his partner, was the truth about his past. He laughs hard about that now. "Yeah, on the first date I reach over and take her hand and say, 'Let me tell you about my sexual abuse.' Nah, I didn't do it that fast."

He did tell her promptly, though, before they were too fully involved, because "concealing," he says, is just another form of lying. He'd done that many times before, and knew it ensured failure.

Concealing is just another form of lying.

He had to admit, too, that much as he wanted a relationship, he was afraid of his track record, and even more frightened of having children.

"I wanted children so much, but I was so worried about what the abuse had done to me. What if it had turned me into an abuser? What if I suddenly became an alcoholic?"

And that's when it comes back to the leap of faith. "Why would I ever, ever, abuse a child when I know how horrific that is? And I don't have a propensity for drinking. I wasn't actually related to my adoptive parents, anyway. Besides, I would not tolerate being that sort of a parent. And I am a good person."

Changing his own life wasn't enough for Dane, though. "Once you feel that it can be different, you want to help make it different for everyone. You want to save as many people as possible from the experience you endured."

Dane's biggest obstacle had been the secrecy and the lies. He had not begun to heal until he found the courage to tell what happened, to speak up. That's why he created a Web site called "Talking Works," now the electronic brain of a burgeoning educational consulting business that raises consciousness about abuse.

"I want to help provide a nurturing and protective place where stories can be shared and where direction toward healing can be given in a trustworthy context."

As so often happens when you finally find the right path in life, his work immediately gathered momentum. "It took on a life of its own," says Dane, who now provides workshops, coaching and motivational speaking.

He spends his most rewarding time communicating, often with young people and other abuse victims, about the benefits of facing your demons—and exorcising them.

On visits to schools, community centres and youth shelters he shares his history and urges others to report their problems and demand the help they deserve.

Talking helps Dane, too, because the more he tells the story of his past, the more he finds he is not alone, and that his experience is shared by many. And his isolation, born of humiliation and the lies he told to hide it, melts away.

"You realize people have had things happen to them, too. We've all had difficult times. And the more I told my story the more the shame dropped away and the more the blathering negative voices in my head disappeared."

His goal now is to "live big" and seek out joy.

"Joy is feeling peaceful. Joy is having a conversation and crying. Connecting with people. Joy is being absolutely honest, no matter what anybody thinks, not taking it personally."

And, then, on May 18, 2003, the unimaginable happened to Doug Dane. He became a father.

Today, joy is knowing that Eden Grace Lucchetta-Dane will have loving parents and a real childhood. Joy is starting over.

ROSE HANDY

*A scholarship student survives rape
and betrayal before discovering
her real path in life.*

S OMETHING IS WRONG with Rose Handy's baby. It refuses
to be born. For two weeks it has teased and tormented her
with contractions, keeping her awake at night and anxious
during the day, and still nothing. It's the dead of winter, and twice
Handy has gone out into the snow to report to the hospital emergency room and twice she's been sent home. Now she's two weeks
past her due date, with pains that come less than five minutes apart
for a while—then stop. Finally, even the doctor loses his patience
and tells Handy, a petite woman with a huge belly, to call a cab: it's
time to induce labour and deliver that stubborn ball of baby.

Stuffed into her parka, suitcase in hand, Handy swings open
the apartment door and calls to the driver to wait a minute. As she

bends down to check she's got everything she'll need, a piece of paper stuck to the door catches her eye. She sees the words "Sheriff" and "Eviction" before tearing it down and stuffing it into her purse, rushing against the ticking meter of the cab. Must be a mistake, she thinks, and makes plans to clear it up as soon as she's settled in the hospital. Handy speaks several languages, works in a Toronto bank and has always been good about meeting deadlines. She knows the baby's father, the man she lives with, has been dutifully delivering her rent money to the landlord each month, so the sheriff has made a mistake.

A couple of hours later, with her contractions intensifying, Handy is sitting on the edge of her hospital bed, holding her head and listening intensely to the woman on the phone at the building management office. There is no mistake: Handy and her boyfriend are behind on the rent and they're being evicted. In fact, no one can understand how Handy even got the keys to the apartment, since nothing but a $100 deposit has ever been paid. They are out, period. Don't come back.

Shocked and rocking on the bed like "a big ball," Handy is speechless. No home for her baby! All her money gone! After all her saving and all her planning!

It is too outrageous to contemplate. Her mind works to knit another version of truth from the same facts. Really, there *has* to be a mistake, a wrong name, misplaced rent receipts. Quickly, she calls her boyfriend's cellphone and when there is no answer, calls him at work. But the company receptionist doesn't recognize his name. Oh, please! What is happening to the world, to her world? The pains bang inside her. Please, she says, check again. This man she's known for several years, whose baby is about to be born, leaves the apartment every morning like clockwork; he's always there when she returns. He works a solid nine-to-five day: please check again; he's there!

Finally, the human resources manager is on the phone. She is calm, and she knows with certainty the names of the people on her payroll. Handy's boyfriend lost his job months ago, about the same time the landlord claims the rent money failed to materialize.

Handy feels sick. The pains, dry and potent, roll on. She revises her "to do" list: find boyfriend, find rent receipts, convince landlord to hold her apartment, have baby; breathe, breathe, breathe.

Swiftly, Handy calls her boyfriend's cellphone again and leaves a message when it rings and rings: Where are you? I am having the baby! Come to the hospital and bring the rent receipts! Now! Hurry!

It is Wednesday. The doctor orders medication to make the baby come; it will not. The boyfriend does not come, either.

On Thursday, when he finally appears, he is carrying a briefcase and reassurances—the sheriff is stupid, the rent is paid and all is well. He is apologetic for her distress and Handy is relieved. But she insists on seeing the receipts. He pulls up a chair by her bed and snaps open his case, leafing through its contents, as she rocks with contractions. He leafs through the papers, looks up, dumbfounded. How could he have forgotten them? They were right there on the desk at home but he forgot to pick them up. That's it! Oh, dear; he'll bring them next visit, really.

With a racing hot panic, Handy watches the pathetic charade. "That's when it hit me. Oh, my God. There is no money, there is nothing."

And it begins to sink in. He's lied. He has no job. There are no receipts because there have never been any payments. He has pocketed all of the money she's given him—for rent, a crib, diapers, baby clothes. Thousands of dollars she worked hard for and went without to save, and the father of her child has taken all of it.

Her head is pounding, her heart is pounding, her stomach is pounding—and inside her, the tiny baby splays its tiny feet and flips, utterly unwilling to emerge. ("I think that was probably a pretty smart decision," Handy will say later.)

Fortunately, one of Handy's sisters is at the hospital, too, although unaware of the domestic crisis. What she does know is that Rose is having a medical crisis and she suspects the boyfriend —she never liked him, anyway—isn't helping the situation. She asks him to leave.

Suddenly, Handy is aware of a buzz around her. Doctors and nurses are shooting in and out of her room, hooking up beeping machines and glancing at her nervously. Apparently, as Handy's life is turning upside down, so is her child, swimming up and away from the birth canal.

"The baby is totally upside down right now. They are all around me and they don't even know what other drama in my life is going on."

And yet Handy says nothing, and reaches out to no one. Shocked, embarrassed, and feeling very alone, she slides into an abyss of hopelessness and wraps it tight around her, like a shawl. *What can they do for me? Nothing. What can anybody do for me? Nothing. I must handle this myself.*

The next day, Saturday, following a full twenty-four hours of hard "pushing," she at last gives birth. After days and days of labour, Handy holds her tiny daughter, Evanna, in her arms and knows that they are utterly alone. She is thousands of miles from home, and a single mother with nowhere to live. She is everything her parents did not want her to be. She is nothing they predicted she'd become.

Handy was born in the West Central African town of Makak, Cameroon, in 1969, the ninth of eleven children. She didn't, as sometimes happens in large families, get lost in the crowd— even as her big-hearted mama swept kids into their home like dust off the street. She was too smart and too full of life for that to happen.

But Handy cannot recall a time when there wasn't somebody extra at the dinner table, or when she wasn't required to run up the path or across the field with a basket of bread or the last of the stew.

"I remember every single day my mother would cook. And was always sharing. Go give here, go give there. Always trying to make people be happy around her."

Handy's father was a respected educator who ran a school, and frequently brought poor children home to live with his family so they'd be able to finish their classes. As an elder, his advice was often sought by the community. Her mother, whose organizational skills kept the huge household fed and happy, would remain the national president of the Presbyterian Church women's collective even at the age of seventy.

So, God lived in Handy's house and had much to say about the way she grew up. Yet those spiritual teachings and the social taboos of her culture would later make it difficult for Handy to turn to her beloved parents precisely when she needed them most.

Her parents were also entrepreneurs who owned several poultry farms. Before even the first tendril of morning light, Handy's parents would gently wake their children and lead them in prayer. Sleepy heads were lightly chastised with Bible proverbs that equate excessive sleep with death, and sloth with sin. But always gently, Handy recalls.

After meditations, Handy would run to the river with her sisters and brothers to fetch water for the chickens. Next she would put on her school clothes—always clean and neat—and then there was breakfast at the big table and noisy predictions for the day ahead. "It was a very lovely childhood. Always laughing, always happy," she says.

In return for God's gifts, much was expected of the children, especially Rose, who was born after two boys in a row and grew up emulating their aggressiveness. "I was trained to *be* something. To be somebody. Every day my father gave us an affirmation that meant 'You will be somebody out of hard work.'"

Handy recalls she always felt competitive. As young as three, she was asked to stand in church and give a "little speech"—even a line or two. She became something of a local celebrity—albeit a miniature one—who won the spelling bees, led class orations and rarely doubted she'd finish anything but first in her class. At nine, she was approached by a successful female politician who told her she was blessed with talent and certain to be a politician like her one day.

At seventeen, Handy won a scholarship to study journalism in France. She left her native country, determined to come back a successful professional. Her parents voiced their expectations loudly and often. Rose was going to make it big!

She already spoke French, the local Bassa language and was also learning Spanish, German and English. Her parents hoped Handy would return as a political journalist, or even a lawyer, and bring the family more honour.

It was not to be.

At first, classes in Tours, an ancient city nestled in the country-side south of Paris, were promising. Handy studied, played hand-ball and occasionally went to the campus nightclub with friends. But in her second year, it all went wrong.

A young student who'd offered to escort her back to her room one night forced himself past her good-night at the door, and raped her. Within two months, she realized he'd also left her preg-nant. She was eighteen years old.

In all the planning for Handy's life, this had never been in the script. She was scared and humiliated. "I couldn't tell anyone. It's something that I had to live with. I was a student alone there and I could not even tell my family."

In Cameroon, as in many other places, single women who become pregnant are often blamed and ostracized, even when they've been sexually assaulted. "In my cultural background, a lot of things are taboo. Back home, you get raped, you do not talk about it."

And back home there was also no room for the choice Handy wanted to make: to terminate the unwanted pregnancy. "In Cameroon, if you get raped, you get pregnant, you will have the baby because abortion is not something that is easy to get."

Unable to face her family with what she believed was failure, and yet unwilling to live out a destiny forced upon her, she anguished over the decision to have an abortion. Her sense of family, her physical fear of the procedure, but mainly the prohibitions of her religion, rubbed her conscience raw. Her mother, especially, was in her mind—the adored matriarch who had given birth to almost a dozen children and always wanted more.

She'd heard her mother's story a thousand times. How she'd lost her own mother at the age of three and how her father had wanted to sell the toddler into marriage immediately. How Handy's great-grandmother had scolded him and then finally snatched away the baby, secretly turning her over to Presbyterian ministers. Handy's mother grew up without a family, a situation she rectified the moment she married.

But Rose Handy was different. She dreamed of ideas and independence, leaning, she says, more toward her father's entrepreneurial spirit than her mother's maternal one. She wanted a family, but not then, not at the age of eighteen. "I had been raised to become someone, to do something. I was not going to be able to do that if I had a baby. I had other things to do first."

She found a therapist and poured out her heart. She discovered two things about herself: she did not want to give birth to a child conceived through rape; and, at that point in her life and unmarried, she did not want to have a baby at all. "It took a lot of sessions with a psychologist to know that I had to have the abortion."

She felt locked inside a puzzle box: if she returned home pregnant, she would disappoint and perhaps anger her parents. If she had an abortion, she would anger her God. She opted to do what she thought was right—terminate the pregnancy and keep it a secret. After almost two decades growing up in her big, noisy, loving family, making that life decision and handling it on her own was the toughest time of her life. She prayed God would forgive her.

"I am alone. My parents are pushing me and I can do no wrong. What else am I going to do? I have to live up to that image. I have to keep on going."

Handy underwent the procedure and then turned to sport to keep her mind busy. It took her a long time to forgive herself, especially as she felt too much guilt to go back to church for a while. She worried a lot and drank to drown it, but she will always believe she made the right choice. And, frankly, she felt tremendous relief: she did what was right for her at that time.

A few months after the abortion, she was pleased to be called into the office of one of her professors.

On the desk, she could see the most recent exam papers. She wondered how well she'd done. Pretty well, it turned out, but the professor was saying something now that made her head spin. She felt sick. She started to sweat.

He was telling her that, despite her good test results, he would be forced to lower her grade if she wasn't—co-operative. At first, she really did not understand what he meant. When his intent became sickeningly clear, she feigned incomprehension.

"He said, 'Oh, come on, you know what I am talking about. If you can be *nice*.' He said he could give me a lower grade if I didn't go out with him, if I didn't sleep with him."

The young woman of whom so much was expected felt ambushed and betrayed.

"I was numb in his office, totally numb. What am I going to do?"

Tell someone? "Back then in France, they will never believe the student. Never."

Lonely for family, feeling like a huge failure and afraid of her professor's threats, Handy decided she had no option but to leave the university, even though that meant abandoning her plans to be a lawyer or a politician. She was in her third year, close to finishing a "diplôme" in business administration.

One of her sisters was living in Paris, and although that sibling would not know for many years what had happened, she immediately offered to help support her. "I didn't want to go to Paris, but I didn't have anywhere else," Handy says.

In 1991, the hard-working scholarship student began her new life: taking courses in public administration at business school five days a week; stripping beds and hauling garbage at a local hotel Friday, Saturday and Sunday.

"You try to push, to put in as many hours as possible to make money. But I hated Paris. It was too big and I wasn't prepared. I didn't go for the right reasons."

Any fantasy of finding a safe haven evaporated. "It's very cold in Paris, unfriendly. Your neighbour when he has to go out would prefer to close his door and wait for you to leave first, so he doesn't have to say 'hello' to you," she says.

And while Handy had felt accepted in the "tolerant" academic community of Tours, Paris in the early 1990s was different for a young woman with a light chocolate complexion.

"There are little things like, you will sit on a subway beside a white person and then just because you are black, they're just going to stand up. They would rather stand than sit beside you."

Her race, she says, also hampered her job search. Despite her university studies, her fluency in French and German (and the beginnings of Spanish and English), she was turned down for every position but babysitting or housekeeping. Employers would agree to interview her based on her résumé, then say *non* when they met her in person.

"You'd go for the interview and then they won't take you. They won't employ you because you're black. And it's all that simple. It was very hard to adjust," she says.

How certain can she be that it was her race and not some other factor—experience or education, for instance—that chased away jobs? She laughs. "They would tell you that they'd *like* to employ you but, truthfully, their clients would leave if they did. So they say, 'I prefer to choose my clients over you, so I cannot hire you, even for a summer job.'"

Yet, Handy chose to see her plight not as a misfortune but as a message, part of a journey she did not yet understand.

"Despite it all, I just felt like I had to keep going. I grew up believing that everything in life happens for a reason. Every time I have a hurdle, I always believe that there is a better thing ahead for me. And that's why I have a hurdle."

Overcoming hurdles is both necessary and is a reward in itself.

Of course, Handy's father had taught her that gain comes through work. "If I look deeper, I will find out what is ahead for me there. So I just have to learn from what I am doing. I believe that God is creating a path for me and I just have to keep my eyes open."

When she prays, Handy says, she asks God to help her be "clairvoyant enough to see the path" that has been chosen for her. "And so every time I go through a challenge, that is God telling me something about where I am going—or not going. If I'm going somewhere but that's not where I should be going, I should look elsewhere."

Handy's faith sustains her when others shun her, feeds her soul where others trammel it. But can the simplicity of her faith, its straightforward eloquence, explain away the uglier aspects of life? Why would God have allowed Rose Handy to be raped?

"Maybe that's a hard one that I cannot answer. But that taught me something about myself, because I look at how far I went after the rape, went beyond the rape. For some people, you get raped and your life is over. Or you get raped and you get a baby and your life is over. Or you go through a lot, having that baby and knowing that you got that baby through a rape. But I was able to make a decision about what was good for me at that point," she says.

"Yes, I got raped, but it is not the end of the world. So I just have to keep on going. As long as I am breathing, I have to keep on going. I can be stronger."

Handy says her reaction to the rape—and the necessity of handling the emotional fallout on her own—unearthed new strength in her. She also grew beyond hating her assailant to simply wiping him from her list of what mattered.

"Putting all my emotions into hating him, it's not important, because that's not about me. I have better things that can come if I don't concentrate on hating that guy, but learn to help myself go past that thing."

That most difficult of lessons—putting one's well-being first —was only in its embryonic phase, however. Handy would be pushed down, held down, several more times before she learned once and for all how to stand up for herself. First, though, she needed somewhere to live that didn't make her sad.

Since childhood, Handy had daydreamed about Canada. At school in Cameroon, she'd read French comic books about the brave settlers of Quebec; two of her sisters had moved to Canada and wrote of opportunity and equality. But Handy was no longer naïve. Certain she'd face similar trouble finding a job in North America, she worked two or three jobs in Paris, saving enough money to ensure she could afford to live while looking for work.

"I do not know what's going to happen when I come to Canada. Am I going to find a job easily? And if I don't get a job, how am I going to be able to pay for my shoes because back then, it was very important for me to have good clothes and good shoes." She'd always been expected to dress and behave respectably; poverty wasn't going to take that from her, she says.

But life in Canada turned out to be far better than she'd hoped. In icy December 1993, Handy temporarily moved into her sister's Toronto apartment and immediately began volunteering to gain experience for her résumé.

"The first morning after I came to Canada, I was walking on the street and someone said 'Hi' to me! I turned around to make sure he was talking to me and I realized I was the only one on the street so he actually was saying 'Hi' to me. I've never been in another city where people accept you like that. That's why I love it here and I am not shy about saying it."

It took more than a year, but she found a fascinating job as a volunteer co-ordinator for OASIS Centre de Femmes, a French-language women's support group that helped victims of assault. That job—and the independence and responsibility that came with it—would provide the backbone for her future.

Then, just as her career began to make sense, her personal life reared up and bit her, hard. To this day, she does not want to speak the name of the man who almost stole her dream again, mainly because she has chosen to forget him.

He was a fellow African who was quiet and sometimes funny. They met in 1994 and when one thing led to another, as it so often does, they moved in together to share the rent.

She found a job at a bank. The relationship never deepened. They had different values and goals; she wasn't going to stay. And then everything changed.

Handy was twenty-seven when she noticed trouble with her menstrual cycle. She bled too much and had too much pain. One doctor diagnosed a miscarriage, but Handy knew this was impossible as she'd been taking birth control pills diligently. Finally, another doctor ordered a full work-up of tests and one of them came back positive. Startlingly, despite the bleeding, she *was* pregnant. More than four months pregnant.

"So, that day was a shock. I say, 'No, no!' I don't even want to hear about having children. Right now, I am nothing and I have nothing. I love children but I would like to be at a certain level and feel that I can provide for them, and take care of them."

Had she been only two months pregnant, Handy says she would have almost certainly elected to have another abortion. She was with the wrong man, at the wrong time, in the wrong place. But with the fetus more than four months old, Handy thought an abortion would be too risky. She also felt that this mysterious occurrence must be a sign. Why else would the pregnancy have progressed so stealthily?

"God didn't want to give me an option. He doesn't want me to do anything about this. There must be a reason why I have to have this baby," she says.

How do you know that when things "go wrong" they aren't actually "going right"?

Determined to give birth to a healthy child, Handy moved into her sister's home, away from the tense relationship with the baby's father. She ate well, worked hard at the bank and only found another apartment and moved back in with her boyfriend when she was almost full-term and certain that all was well with the pregnancy. She did so reluctantly.

"For the first time in my life, I listened to people while making a personal decision. They're telling me, 'Oh, you're better off with the father around.' All those things they say to women, just to scare them off," she says.

But Handy devoted herself to her new family, sending the father off to buy baby supplies and deliver the money she'd saved to pay the rent, while she fussed over a nest for the newborn.

What she would not know until she was in the hospital and racked with labour pains, was that her boyfriend was the last person in the world she should have trusted.

As she holds her small Evanna in her arms, just hours after giving birth, she is fascinated and filled with a mighty fortitude. Everything, she realizes, has changed, must change. She has never felt more alone, yet she has never felt more determined.

"I was going to do everything to protect her. No more mistakes. No more compromising. I was all she had and that was going to be enough."

Sometimes we learn to protect someone else first.

From the telephone by her hospital bed, Handy persuaded her landlord to allow her to stay in the apartment a few more weeks. When her boyfriend reappeared, threatening to have someone come after their baby unless he was permitted to move back in, she called the police. They eventually picked him up and asked her what she wanted done.

"I said, 'Actually, all I want is for him to get out of here, get out of my apartment, leave me alone, leave my daughter alone and not come near us and not touch anything that concerns me or my daughter. Just go away.'"

And so it was that Handy, still waiting for her maternity leave insurance cheque to arrive, found herself penniless and very alone with a hungry baby.

She insists she was not afraid. "I couldn't give him the satisfaction. It would have been good for him to see me down. There's no way I could give that to him because this is the guy who's putting me through hell and I didn't do anything. I was everything to him, good to him. I didn't deserve this. I'm not going to allow this to affect me. It's just that simple."

Angry, scared and still weak from her ordeal, Handy spent hours telephoning overcrowded women's shelters.

Finally, with her daughter in her arms and a few possessions in a bag, she was shown to the last room in the last shelter, and found it blessedly empty. "So when I want to cry I can stay there and cry on my own."

She desperately needed rest. "I was breast-feeding my child 100 percent and I was not feeding myself properly and I was going through tremendous stress. I was so tired," she recalls.

"But at the same time I needed to keep making my daughter feel secure. I was always told that they feel through breast milk when you're under a lot of stress. And I could feel that at one point when she would be crying while I was breast-feeding her. It was killing me inside."

Her child was drinking in her mother's silent pain and wailing it out.

Rather than resenting her time in the shelter, Handy was grateful, and made the most of her temporary support. "I was just so relieved to have a place to stay that was safe. I felt like all my plans that I'd worked so hard on were taken from me. I needed to get myself together again."

But ask Handy whether she is a hero and she'll shake her head in a vehement no. Point out her courage and she'll set you straight. It's not courage that helped her survive, but lack of it.

"I am very good at hiding it but I think I am very fragile. Being fragile is not a weakness for me. Actually, it is a strength. It is my biggest strength."

Sometimes your "flaw" can be the source of your strength.

It may not be the most obvious logic, but it's a formula that works well for Handy. "I had a good friend who always told me that no matter how bad a situation gets, you can always dig deeper in yourself to find a strength to move forward," she explains. "Knowing I'm fragile is the biggest strength that I can have, because as a fragile person I have to try harder, I know I have to find a way to dig even deeper into myself than another person so I can move forward."

She knows it may be difficult for some people to understand what she means, but that doesn't matter. When something works for you, it works. Don't question it; don't discount it—just grab it and go, she says.

So, once she regained her strength in the shelter, Handy analyzed her situation and immediately decided that a regular nine-to-five job wouldn't work any more. There wouldn't be enough money left over for daycare, and she felt an overwhelming need to protect her child. "I realized my reality now was that I was a single parent. I had to start a business. I have special skills. I could put them to my benefit."

Trained in business and human resources, with a special ability to communicate with people—and several languages in which to do it—Handy set her sights on launching a magazine for francophone racial minorities in Canada, particularly those who were having difficulties in their new country.

Each day, she'd pack up her baby and head to the library to do research, or she'd spend hours scouring the book collection at the women's shelter.

Eventually, she concluded her dream was too expensive and too risky. But her digging had turned up something else: Canadian companies, especially in Toronto, were in need of a service that could help them find bilingual workers. Handy decided to create one. She realized that such an organization could, at the same time, provide support for new immigrants.

Handy says *Bilingual Link* is the first innovative online service that offers superior human-resources solutions; it promotes career development and bilingual opportunities in jobs, careers, training and services. Five years later, her company helps match bilingual employees with jobs—coaching them and helping with résumé writing, while also assisting employers find and keep the right staff.

She also publishes *Jobs & Carrières Infos*, an employment newspaper filled with bilingual job opportunities. She still gets a rush when she sees it stacked on the counter in employment and community agencies, or in schools and churches and libraries.

"I just discovered a little niche of people who speak French. Some just get here or have been here looking for work and don't know how to go about finding out what opportunities are there for bilingual people. And some of them do not even know there's a huge francophone community here."

So, against all odds, Rose Handy launched her consulting and employment firm while she was homeless. "People say I can't do this or I can't do that because things aren't right yet, but I learned the hard way that things are the way they are, so they are probably right for you now. Just keep going."

Just keep going.

Handy appreciated the irony of her situation. She was still living in the shelter when she landed her first big contract as a conference organizer for a non-profit group working to help francophone women get ahead. She used the shelter as her office, the public library as her resource centre, and set out on the morning of her first big consulting job pushing Evanna in her stroller.

"They were having workshops and I was co-ordinating the whole thing. They didn't know while I was sitting there the whole time that I came from the shelter and after the workshop I went back to the shelter."

Several years later, while looking through old photographs with her daughter, Evanna, Handy found a picture from the conference. She could not stop staring at it, knowing that it represented a huge personal victory. She pointed to the hopeful-eyed woman in the middle of the workshop and promised her puzzled little daughter that one day she would explain to her why this image meant so very much.

When Evanna is old enough, Handy says, she will also tell her about the struggle of their early life together. And if her daughter worries that her mother's accidental pregnancy crippled her dreams, she will learn this truth: "Evanna is the reason behind everything I am today and everything I will ever be."

Handy says she would likely have stayed on a slow slide into mediocrity had she not become pregnant with her daughter.

"It was getting very easy to forget about why I came to Canada in the first place. It's very easy to get into that life. You have that low-life boyfriend who is just sitting there, and all you are doing is trying to manage to live with him. You have a little job where maybe you go to work in a call centre. And then you have your little income to pay for your rent. And you pay for your clothes and you're just sitting there."

Before you know it, Handy warns, you forget who you wanted to be; the voices of your proud, prodding parents die away, and life loses its potential.

"Bit by bit, you're surrounded by people living the same pattern, and you forget that you *know* you can accomplish greater things."

Don't let anyone pull you off your course.

Handy may have been close to capitulating, surrendering her dreams, compromising her own well-being, but from the first moment she held Evanna, she knew she'd never settle for second-best for her daughter.

"My parents raised me to accomplish special things, and that's not what I was doing with my life. That's why I always believe that God wanted me to have Evanna, so I would wake up and realize that what I was heading into was not the life for me."

VINCE SAVOIA

*A paramedic endures five paralyzing years of
post-traumatic stress disorder after attending
to a beautiful murder victim, yet emerges
an even bigger hero on the other side.*

NEAR THE END OF HIS SHIFT, Toronto paramedic Vince
Savoia gets the call from dispatch. "See the police on
scene." The instruction is vague, tersely worded, with
suspiciously little information.

But Savoia understands police-radio minimalism. He spent
three years as an emergency dispatcher himself, trying to keep
police reporters off the scent. A message as cryptic as this means
they're probably being called to something bad—a domestic or
homicide, most likely homicide.

So, minutes before the end of that long day—January 27,
1988—Savoia and his partner jump into their ambulance and

rush to a high-rise apartment in downtown Toronto, jabbing at the elevator button for the twenty-second floor.

And that's where Savoia's clear recollection slides into fog. To tell his story, he must tell it slowly.

He remembers knocking on the door, and being met by a police officer, who is very shaken up. His colour is grey. His only words, "She's in the bedroom."

Inside, Savoia and his partner exchange looks; the cop's ominous tone and the peculiar atmosphere in the upscale apartment register on both their spines. It isn't the first death they have attended, but it's odd. Normally at the scene of a homicide or any act of violence, there are signs of struggle. This place is absolutely immaculate. Something strange has happened here.

The officer leads Savoia and his partner into the bedroom.

At once they see the outline of a body, the murder victim. She's lying on the bed, with the sheets pulled up over her head.

Savoia peels away the linen to reveal a naked battered body, and his head and limbs crackle with shock. He is staring straight into the lifeless face of his fiancée.

Mirella Conte, the girl he'd admired from afar in grade school, then finally asked out as a young man. They had been dating for years and had finally set a date. And now, here she is: colour drained away, hair dishevelled, badly beaten. Gone.

Vince Savoia is the eldest son of a restaurateur who sold his famous spicy sandwiches at College and Clinton Streets in the heart of Toronto's Little Italy. Growing up, Savoia was a "good Italian boy," went to church, nurtured his sensitive side with music lessons, and at the age of ten began working the busy Saturday shift at San Francesco's, wrapping hundreds of veal and tomato sauce sandwiches for his father's customers. He was well paid and well fed and he liked sliding the fat, fragrant packages into eager hands. Life was good.

But when Vince was fifteen, his father suffered a nervous breakdown. To help pay the mortgage and buy groceries, Vince gave music lessons three or four days a week after school.

He kept close tabs on his two younger sisters, too. He'd been taught early that women were to be cherished and protected. "I was brought up to always treat any girl I dated like she was my sister. So, I never liked playing the field. I always had that sort of respect."

As a boy, Savoia loved the television show *Emergency*, which was all about strong, cocky men who thought fast, moved fast, and saved lives in every episode. His attraction to the show made sense. After all, Savoia had always been in the business of helping people—his fragile father, his weary mother and, for a good chunk of their lives, his sisters. Hero. He liked the job description.

"You're there when people in trouble need you most and you're properly trained and you can get them to medical aid. It feels really good to be able to help," he says.

But Savoia's first emergency call as a twenty-one-year-old student paramedic didn't stick to the television script. The address was in Toronto's Jane-Finch neighbourhood, well known then for its drug trade and gangs. His stomach was tense, his senses prickly, as he and his two senior paramedic colleagues sped to a house fire. A crowd was straining through the caustic smoke pluming from seared wood and melted plastic. Savoia felt a thrill: this was what he'd been trained to do!

"You're doing CPR and you're using a bag valve mask, trying to resuscitate a patient. Your adrenaline is running and you really don't think about it while you're doing the call because you're there to do a job, right?"

But no human skill, however sharply honed, could save the toddler that night, his lungs filled with ashes.

So, on his first mission as a paramedic-in-training, six years before the fateful homicide call in 1988, Savoia was no one's hero, just a guy carrying a tiny corpse on a big stretcher into the hospital. As he drove home, he was enveloped by waves of sadness. And later, there would be flashbacks and the whip-tip of panic. Not a lot, he's quick to add even now. "I would see this child's face in my mind. You can't put yourself in the parents' shoes, but the empathy kind of poured out and I was really, really sad that we had this opportunity to hopefully save a three-year-old, but we just couldn't."

So, what did he and his fellow emergency workers do with the distress or pain that frequently comes after a disturbing call? Usually, they just pretended it didn't affect them.

Back at the shop the next day, comparing notes with colleagues, he discovered that most had spent that first night of their careers on "routine transfers," ferrying patients from one hospital to another—well-trained drivers working for a shuttle service.

When Savoia told them, "You know, I had someone who passed away last night," there was silence and then jokes. "To relieve the pressure, because if you dwell on it too long, it would just drive you crazy," he explains.

It would take the homicide call and five lost years to teach Savoia that it's not the talking that drives you nuts, it's the *not talking*.

Vince Savoia is horror-struck and helpless as he stares at the corpse of the woman he'd chosen to be his wife.

"When I first looked at the victim she had an extreme resemblance to Mirella. So for a split second, I thought it *was* my fiancée lying on that bed. She could have been her twin sister."

Even their names had a similar sound to Savoia's keen ear: Tema Conter and Mirella Conte. *Kon-ter and Kon-tay.* Conte and

Conter. *Kon-tay and Kont-ter.* "It shook me up. You get that shake, that sugar bolt. It was a split second and then you forget about it. You are there to do a call."

Conter had suffered multiple stab wounds. That's all Savoia will tell you at first. Sixteen years later, he cannot—will not—describe all of what he saw in the woman's bedroom. Terror. Denial. Respect. He felt it all for the young murder victim.

Media reports of the crime are less sentimental. The dark-haired, twenty-five-year-old had been stabbed eleven times, all over her nude body. Brutally raped. Bound hand and foot and gagged, which explains why there were no signs of a struggle in her apartment.

"It was the first time I had seen something that vicious. You wonder how any human being can do this to another human being," Savoia says. "And you wonder what sort of terror went through her mind in her final moments. Because she was bound and gagged and helpless. She couldn't defend herself. You have a sense of anger toward the person who did this. And you feel help-less because there's nothing that you can do."

There is a nightstand by the bed and on it a telephone. "I think we better call the coroner because there's nothing we can do here," he tells his partner. He reaches for the phone. A police officer shouts at him to put it down. In his panic, Savoia has violated one of the best-known rules of a crime scene. "Obviously, the last thing you want to do is tamper with the evidence, so you don't touch anything. But I wanted to help." Fortunately, he is wearing gloves.

Tema Conter's murderer, a convicted rapist out on a tempo-rary pass and staying at a nearby halfway house, will eventually be caught and sentenced to life in prison.

But Vince Savoia will never be the same. "The innocence died that day. It changed my life in that I just don't take anything for granted any more. She was a victim of a random act of violence, and it could happen to any of us at any given time." His encounter with this random act also sets in motion an insidious mental illness that will plague him for years.

Back at the ambulance hall, Savoia strips off his uniform, and as he drives home, he cries. "The tears just flowed because she was helpless and there wasn't anything we could do."

When Savoia walks through his front door and finds his fiancée waiting there for him, safe and sound, he breaks down again. "I just let out this flood of emotion because she was okay, but on the flip side it could have been her who was that victim instead of Tema Conter."

It could have been her.

It could have been her.

It could have been her.

Savoia can't shake the mad jig in his head.

"For a few days after the call, I would wake up with sweats and tremors and flashbacks. And the scary part is that whenever I shut my eyes the only thing I saw was Tema Conter lying on the bed, and feeling very helpless and very guilty that I wasn't able to be there and help her or save her life. We were too late."

For eight months in 1988, Savoia was treated by a staff psychologist for trauma. He tried to get on with his life: he and Mirella married in July, 1989. But the romance backfired; now that she was his wife, Savoia's paranoia returned with new energy. He began to have nightmares even while he was awake.

Look!

There was Tema Conter opening her apartment door. There was Melvin Stanton, the man who would rape and kill her, skulking in the corridor. There she was, all fresh and eager for work, being dragged from the hall before she could reach the elevator. In broad daylight, on a day like any other. There she was, pleading, but no one could hear.

Savoia's paranoia became so intense he couldn't bear his wife going outdoors without him. "I was obsessed with my wife's safety. I didn't want her to leave home. Even during the day if she had to go buy milk at the corner store, that would petrify me. I was afraid she'd be another victim. I was afraid I wouldn't be there to help."

At the height of his distress, Savoia tried to forbid his wife to leave the house or use the car. "I had to see her in front of me all the time. Whenever I lost sight of her I would get the shakes and the tremors."

Of course, he had to go to work, but Savoia says he really cannot remember much of 1989 except his wedding day. "I wasn't happy, very depressed obviously. Very stressed. I was just in a state of emotional limbo."

So he shook and he hid and he ate, gaining more than seventy pounds in less than two years. Even wrapped in 300 pounds of flesh, he couldn't block the memories. He couldn't sleep. He couldn't concentrate. He was constantly afraid he'd get sent out on another homicide call.

The birth of the couple's first child in 1990, a daughter, only made Savoia more anxious. "You start thinking, Can it happen to her? How will I protect her? As a father, you want to make sure that nothing happens to your child." The mantra amplified.

It could happen to her.

It could happen to her.

It could happen to both of them.

He was plagued with doubts and began to second-guess everything about his life. Why did they have a child? Was it right to bring a child into this world, where she would never be safe? Most of all, it was "terrifying" to him that he now had another female to protect. What if he failed?

Yet Savoia continued to tell himself that his turmoil was the price he had to pay as an emergency worker—punch the clock, bury the paranoia, pull on the uniform, hide the fear, punch the clock, suck in the grief.

Fortunately for Savoia, though, his much-loved bride threatened to leave him. *Her* price for staying was a second round of counselling. He agreed, and it was there that Savoia finally connected the dots. "I realized that what I was doing, trying to isolate my wife and child, was totally unrealistic, on the verge of being psychopathic almost. I had to change."

––––––––––––––––

Savoia had known all along that he'd suffered a psychological blow at the murder scene. The split second in which he'd mistaken Tema Conter for his young fiancée had triggered a psychological disorder. Doctors even had a name for it—critical incident stress. It's often suffered by emergency service personnel who struggle with the effects of *responding* to tragedy, but with no ability to prevent or stop it. Witness grief. Bystander anxiety. Savoia had a textbook case: experiencing *or witnessing death, serious injury or its threat and, as a result, feeling intense fear, helplessness or horror.*

"I had a tremendous feeling of guilt that I wasn't able to help Tema. That just grew. I felt really bad that I wasn't able to save her life," Savoia says.

When symptoms persist beyond a few months, doctors generally diagnose a case of post-traumatic stress disorder (PTSD). Savoia suffered from both disorders, and exhibited almost every symptom: nightmares, flashbacks, insomnia, hypervigilance, intense psychological distress rising to panic when faced with similar or symbolic events, and avoidance of certain thoughts, places or people that triggered recollection of the trauma.

After the initial counselling, though, Savoia figured he had shrugged it off. He felt better. He didn't appreciate the tenacity of the condition. What he thought was just post-wedding protectiveness and perhaps a mood disorder was full-blown PTSD.

Of course, this reaction is not inevitable. Savoia's partner, who had even less experience on the job when they attended the Tema Conter murder together, recovered more quickly from the horror. He wasn't engaged to a woman who looked just like the victim.

Talk therapy with a trained professional was critical to Savoia's recovery. "You're trying to connect the dots, understand what's making you upset, but you're the main character in this play, so it's tough to see," he recalls.

All along, his wife insisted that it was her resemblance to the murder victim and the trauma of that call that lay at the root of his persistent paranoia, but Savoia rejected that theory for years.

"I had already had treatment for that! I would think she was absolutely crazy. She wasn't there, right? She wasn't my partner. There's no way she can know how I felt. But she knew and I wasn't listening. I wasn't hearing her," he says.

Listen. Someone in your life may be able to connect the dots for you.

With the help of a therapist, Savoia says, he was eventually brought back from the brink of "insanity," able at last to appreciate how bizarre his behaviour had become. And the birth of his second child in April, 1994—another girl—made that recovery even more critical.

"I had to change, and I realized I had to change. I think the connection was coming to understand that a lot of my feelings were based on me feeling guilty for not being able to help. It was an unrealistic feeling. There wasn't anything I could have done. Even if I was the best emergency room doctor."

Indeed, an autopsy showed that by the time Savoia and other emergency personnel reached Conter, she had been dead at least eight, perhaps ten hours. "It took me a long time to really understand that piece of the puzzle. You know, no matter how much I wanted to help Tema, there was nothing I could have done. Yet the overwhelming sense of guilt was the key," he says.

But recovery, like grief itself, is a highly personal experience. If we live differently and experience differently, it makes no sense that our recovery will be the same. For Savoia, still in many ways the young boy raised to honour women and protect his family, therapy would not be enough to quiet his conscience.

Grief and recovery are highly individual experiences.

It did help Savoia to join Toronto Emergency Services' first critical incident stress (CIS) debriefing team as a peer counsellor, offering help to people like himself. Not only did that answer his need to help others, it allowed him to assert some control over his own debilitating CIS symptoms. "Now I was in the position where I could help other peers—not just paramedics, but firefighters and police officers—deal with their feelings when they went to a call that disturbed them. Everybody who has done this job for any length of time will have that one call that has just completely traumatized them.

"I was able to channel my emotions into the proper places and I found that to be extremely helpful in the healing process."

Helping others can transform our pain into someone else's progress.

Finally, four years after his first therapist made the suggestion, Savoia planted a mulberry bush in front of his North York home. It was meant to honour Tema Conter's passing. The memorial blossomed and bore the best fruit anyone had tasted. Savoia was buoyed. When he moved to Bolton, Ontario, in 1997, he brought the tree along and transplanted it. Within days, it was dead.

Savoia was stunned. "I know it was just a tree. It wasn't a person. But it hit me hard."

It took time, but Savoia realized his despair at losing the tree had a meaning beyond the obvious symbolic loss: a fruit tree never would have been enough to sustain Conter's memory, anyway. He wouldn't be satisfied until he'd created a lasting memorial, to guarantee that her goodness outlived the evil done, to ensure that in death she received the respect stolen from her in the final moments of her life.

So, he set out to do what he knew how to do: respect his own personal moral code and lay Tema Conter to rest the way he would a member of his family—a sister, perhaps. "I wanted to honour her. I wanted her to live on. I wanted her death not to have been in vain."

> *Inability to let go may mean it isn't*
> *yet time. Honour your loss.*

In 2000, Savoia launched the Tema Conter Memorial Trust, which today sponsors scholarships, helps educate emergency workers about critical incident stress and post-traumatic stress disorder, and recognizes the media's role in educating the public about mental health issues. Most importantly, the trust and its burgeoning membership fight the social stigma attached to the expression of strong emotion, such as fear and depression. Annual scholarships awarded across Canada for the best essays about post-traumatic disorders help spread awareness among up-and-coming professionals. "Education is the key," Savoia says.

Every year, hundreds of people, including police officers, paramedics and other emergency service personnel, attend an exuberant Valentine's Gala in Tema Conter's memory, celebrating her life and raising money to help the people who tried so hard to help her and others like her.

There was one more thing Savoia wanted to do. He wanted to reach out to Conter's family in Halifax, Nova Scotia, and let them know that her death really did matter to people in Ontario. But he put it off, frightened that he might be intruding on their grief. He didn't want to add to *their* trauma. The idea of connecting, though, just would not go away.

Finally, through a friend who contacted an acquaintance of the family, Savoia received permission to telephone the Conter family. He was surprised to discover that not only was Tema's brother a physician, he also deeply understood and appreciated Savoia's affliction.

Now, Dr. Howard Conter and his wife, Karen, host a twin fund-raising memorial event in Halifax every other year. Together, Savoia and the Conter family are changing the way emergency service people are seen and treated across the country.

"It is so like my sister Tema that even in death, she could unite us to do something so beneficial. She was such a beautiful person and we will be forever grateful to Vince for helping us make something good out of something so horrific," Dr. Conter says.

To this day, it is difficult for Savoia to wholeheartedly regret his struggle; but for his suffering there would be no education program, no memorial, no progress.

But Savoia isn't one to exaggerate: educating the younger generation of emergency workers, especially the men, about the psychological stress of their work is an uphill battle. Savoia says he sees a huge reluctance to admit that shock, anxiety and horror are acceptable and even healthy responses to traumatic experiences.

He makes it a point to speak to college students every year, warning them what they are in for. "They're all young. They're all eager. And they just don't understand that critical incident stress exists. They think it will happen to someone else. They think, It won't happen to me."

Part of the problem, Savoia says, is the age-old myth that masculinity and courage are synonymous with being unemotional, that "feelings" are the hallmark of weakness. "Macho men don't cry, you know? They don't let things worry them. They can handle anything."

But the truth is, it takes far more courage and strength to *experience* emotion than to hide it, a lot more guts to handle the full spectrum of human reaction than to smother it with alcohol, food or other abusive behaviours. Critical incident stress and post-traumatic stress disorder are, in fact, normal reactions to abnormal events, he says.

> **Don't deny that intense experience has changed you or your reality; understand how it has.**

But how many days, weeks, months—years?—does it take to vanquish the memories? In truth, for Savoia, no amount of eating, screaming or talking could completely chase away that dreadful day.

So he stopped trying.

"If I think of Tema, the flashback will come. It's in my memory bank. It'll be there forever. I can't fight that and now I won't. I've learned to respect that image. It's normal."

Rather than bury the image, respect it. Rather than deny the way experience has changed your reality, understand it. You are not *diminished* by trauma or grief. You are enlarged by it. You are bigger, you are stronger, because of your unique experience.

> **Respect memories; don't try to bury them.**

About a year after Savoia established the Tema Conter Memorial Trust, his wife was stunned to discover that, at forty, she was pregnant again. On March 3, 2003, Savoia held his third daughter in his arms.

"I will always be worried about them. I will always want to protect them. I understand now that they must live in the world, too. I can teach them how to be careful, but I do not hold their fate in my hands. I can only do the best I can."

JAENE CASTRILLON

Shunned for her mixed Chinese-Colombian heritage, weight and mental health problems, a young student turns to prostitution and finds her voice to fight for others.

I N THE MIDDLE of the vast Toronto airport, sixteen-year-old Jaene Castrillon's panties are falling out of her rice cooker. Customs officers are combing through her suitcase, emptying plastic bags and unfurling blouses. She's finally home after eight years in Hong Kong, but now everything she owns is spread out before strangers.

"They go through everything. My mom has a knack for packing a lot of stuff in a small suitcase. I had no clue. So they open the rice cooker and there are pens and erasers, socks and underwear. I'm thinking: 'Oh, my God, I am such an immigrant.' It took me so long to pack everything again."

Except she wasn't an immigrant. Castrillon was born in Toronto, and lived there until the age of eight. For years she had begged for permission to return, longing to leave behind the crowds and chaos of Hong Kong, the endless badgering of her relatives, and worst of all, the groping hands of a relative.

But now that she had arrived, clutching her bulging bag and inhaling the stale metal air of the airport, she suddenly felt very alone.

And she was. Although distant friends of her mother would finally find the tired girl with the big bag and deliver her to a borrowed room in Toronto, Castrillon's self-confidence wouldn't last long.

Within months she'd be prescribed medication for depression, and then institutionalized. At the height of her young "career," the smart teen, so quick at math and so good at thinking on her feet, would instead of training as an accountant or lawyer be turning tricks as a prostitute in Toronto's seediest districts.

"I was sad. I probably was having a little bit of challenge adjusting. But I think you have to take that in context. I'm sixteen. I'm away from my family; I had no family or friends. Everything's new. I'm working. I'm going to school."

Problems, though, were piling up faster than Castrillon could solve them. In 1992, she says, Toronto schools would not recognize her Chinese high school diploma, and officials insisted she enroll in English-as-a-second-language courses because of her accent and occasionally faltering grammar. But the ESL instructor kicked her out because she didn't need the remedial help. The girl who left Hong Kong because she "never fit in" did not belong here, either.

And the girl who endured ridicule from relatives "for not being Asian enough" found herself playing the role of demure hostess at a dim sum restaurant, pushing her cart and plying her dumplings.

Despite her good grades she would never get her diploma. Despite her mother's dream of a daughter with a professional career, she would never finish university. And while selling sex seems a distant nightmare for a shy girl, still a virgin, it turned out to be a fairly short journey for someone whose body had often made her the target of contempt.

It would be a long, long time before Castrillon would feel welcome in her native land.

As a child, Jaene Castrillon woke up most mornings to the feeling of loneliness and the sight of three little piles of food: breakfast, lunch and dinner. The front-door key was tied to her lunch box. This was her reassurance that her mother had been home sometime during the night, her feet aching from waitressing, to sleep a few hours before pushing on to her factory job.

"So I'd go to school and take care of myself and then some nights I would go to bed and she still wasn't home. I was six."

Her father, a Colombian immigrant with a drug problem and little sense of responsibility, she says, rarely made it back to their tiny house in Toronto's east end, or wherever the family was living that month.

But little Jaene (pronounced Jane-ee) Castrillon, even at six, was disciplined. She kept herself in line. After school she came straight home, walking the short distance on her own. She served herself and her teddy bear from the dinner pile, talking aloud as she scripted both sides of their conversation (a childhood habit that would later chill her psychiatrists).

Next, her homework must be done. Her mother, who had little faith in a non-Asian education system, expected Castrillon to plow through the extra mathematics books she carried home from the Chinese market. Only after that would the child permit herself an hour or so of television.

Not until she was an adult would Castrillon appreciate that her mother never actually monitored her as a child; that she wasn't home and therefore could not *see* what she was doing. "I didn't figure that out at the time. I thought, 'She's my mom, she'll know.'"

There was the stinging bamboo stick to keep in mind, too. Like her parents before her, Castrillon's mother wielded it fiercely and freely.

"When I was younger, before anybody else started doing multiplication, in her opinion I needed to know my multiplication, so she'd come home and say, 'What's five times five?' Whack. So you had to know your stuff."

Other nights, when the little girl wasn't feeling quite so tough, she curled up on the hard floor, hoping to hear her mother's footfall. "I would sleep in the hallway, waiting for her, because I wanted to at least see her. It wasn't a matter of her being around, but just to see her before I went to bed would have been nice."

Most days, though, Castrillon says she didn't mind her solitude. "I think I liked being alone a bit. I liked not getting too involved, just being by myself and not having to worry about anything." Not surprising, given how much she had to worry about as the daughter of new immigrants, who were struggling with language, ethnicity, money and their own relationship.

When her parents met, her father was working as a short-order cook in the back of a Toronto restaurant, her mother as a waitress in the front. He was recently arrived from Colombia, she from Hong Kong, just seventeen and on her own. They married and had Jaene in 1975, but neither stayed home much.

"The truth is my father was high and drunk a lot. I remember him having hangovers and swearing in Spanish. But I never really thought of him differently 'cause when you're a kid that's your parent and you think everybody's parents are kind of the same." Nor did she have much time to bond with her mother. "My mother wanted me to have a better life so she went and bought a house, which was a little beyond her means and she had three jobs."

Being alone was often much better than being with her parents, anyway. Both yelled at her and both hit her, she says. "My dad used basically whatever was around." On good days that was something soft, on bad days something that really hurt, like a plastic slipper.

Looking back, Castrillon can recognize all the signs of addiction in her father. "It would have explained the emotional rollercoaster. One minute he'd yell at you and the next minute he'd be sobbing an apology."

His drug and alcohol problems also, she says, accounted for his frequent disappearances, as he likely tried to keep a step ahead of crooks and cops. "I never quite understood that. There were periods where I didn't even remember that people had fathers and then he'd show up and I'd think, 'Oh, you're my dad, aren't you?'"

At least her mother was more predictable, Castrillon says, with all her rules and the bamboo stick she used to enforce them. "I always knew that's something I shouldn't talk about because I didn't want to be taken away."

A social worker did visit her home once, after someone noticed cane marks on the little girl. After that, Castrillon's mother avoided hitting her child's tender arms and legs. "She learned not to use the bamboo stick all over, just on the palm where you can't see the marks."

No one, it seems, realized how much time the little girl spent on her own. From doctors years later, Castrillon would learn words such as "abuse, deprivation and abandonment," and from social workers, labels such as "latch-key kid." She would remember the little key tied to her lunch box.

Yet, then as now, anyone who made the mistake of criticizing her mother got a tongue-lashing. She's quick to point out her mother was just twenty-one and all alone when her daughter was born.

"You can't judge her without the context. She tried, she really did, but she had a factory job, waitressing. She was sleeping four hours a day herself."

And worse was on its way.

Castrillon's fractious parents finally separated and in 1984 her mother took Jaene to Hong Kong. The isolation in Canada was replaced by a new emotional and cultural claustrophobia. "It was big. A lot more people. Dirty. I remember garbage everywhere. I hated it."

And rather than finding comfort in the bosom of her extended family, the eight-year-old confronted xenophobia and sexist attitudes. "I didn't feel part of the family. There was a lot of tension and animosity. There were generations of dysfunction even before I came. To top it off, I didn't fit in."

While her relatives were proud of the fact she'd been born in Canada, a country they considered privileged, she says they despised the Latin genes "tainting" her Chinese heritage, darkening her complexion and thickening her thighs. She recalls her relatives' reaction: "I'm overweight. Definitely not a good thing, and I am a 'tomboy.' It was the worst thing you could be. You're supposed to be the docile female, size zero, do music, typing, accounting, girly stuff, find a man of your class, marry him, have babies."

Although Castrillon was of average weight, she didn't have a tiny Asian frame, and the pressure to become physically smaller became unbearable. "Losing weight was a constant issue. I was always told, 'You're fat. You're fat. You're fat. Nobody's going to marry you if you stay fat.' It's the Asian thing. I was on a diet since I was five."

While she struggled to shrink her body, her physical space was disappearing, too. At one point, she was sharing a tiny apartment with her mother, grandmother, grandfather, an uncle and three aunts. She slept in the living room, usually with three other family members. Her mother and grandfather fought frequently about how to run the family's clothing business.

"My grandfather would bring up the fact that my mother was divorced and that she'd married someone not in her culture and I was a half-breed. It was implied quite clearly that she was a bit of a disgrace."

Jaene was their emotional punching bag. "I got most of the verbal lashings. They never hit me. My mom was the only one who did that, but they put so much stress on her that it happened more frequently."

Unwelcome, unsuitable, unpleasing. Eventually, Castrillon evolved from a sweet little girl fearful of risking her mother's disapproval into a teenager determined not to flinch.

"It just got to the point that I thought, 'Whatever. Bring it on, I don't care. It doesn't hurt that much.' I'd cry before, though—you do the pity thing. You cry first and then, when it doesn't work, you say, 'Okay, I'll take it.' You just deal with it. It doesn't even hurt after a while."

She remembers withdrawing emotionally, to protect herself. "It's almost like you just go into a different headspace. I am the queen of disassociating."

Is this the point at which some of Castrillon's psychological problems began to develop, or was it much earlier, when she came home to nothing and went to sleep alone, talking to herself and her stuffed animal? To this day, she says, much of her childhood is a blur, some events recalled, others lost—or pushed away.

Years later when she was locked up in a hospital psychiatric ward, she'd have flashbacks as pieces of the puzzle materialized and then washed away. She is no longer interested in chasing the wispy threads of her memory fabric; she doesn't really want to uncover more abuse. What she does remember, though, is that one of the few friends she found in the family, a male relative, betrayed her, too.

At first, he seemed to love his little relation, playing with her, bringing her treats as soon as she arrived in Hong Kong. "He was very doting, took care of me, babysat me. The first few years, he was the sweetest guy in the world."

Then his behaviour changed dramatically. He had already begun to act strangely—photographing her while she slept, or picking the lock on the bathroom door and snapping a photograph while she was in the shower. She'd hear the door and see the flash of the camera bulb. "But he'd always joke, 'Oh, there's no film. I just did it as a joke.' And people would let him," she says.

One day, however, while she lay on the living-room floor, he was suddenly on top of her, pinning her down and pressing himself against her. Just eleven or twelve, and totally baffled, she pretended to be sleeping under her blanket. Then he was gone.

Afterward, he refused to speak directly to her, referring to the girl in the third person. He began to criticize her clothes and accuse her of promiscuity. "If I wore a tank top, he'd say to my mother, 'Look at your daughter. She's wearing skimpy clothes. She's going to sell her flesh on the street.'" Years later, Castrillon remembered those words as she toyed with the idea of joining the sex trade. "I was already there, right?"

Yet Castrillon told no one what he'd done, not certain whether his behaviour was wrong, just that it made her "extremely uncomfortable."

Castrillon's only sanctuary was the international private school in Hong Kong where instruction was in English and where she excelled. But in retaliation against his rebellious daughter and "half-breed" granddaughter, her grandfather refused to pay her tuition past grade six. Castrillon was forced into one of the roughest schools in Hong Kong. Unable to read and write the language, she found herself unwelcome at home and out of place at school. Violence was tolerated in both places, she says.

"In Hong Kong, the teachers wouldn't even care if you went into school and you were beat up. It's so common there. You compare horror stories. 'This happened last night. I got caught red-handed. My brother totally ratted out and I got the whipping of a lifetime.' So it was normal."

School proved to be a risky refuge. To win the protection of gang members, including heavy hitters in the local Triads, the tough girl got tougher.

"Nobody really gave me too much stress, but I learned things, like how to pickpocket." And her body, always different from typical Asian children, became even more distinct in adolescence.

"I was well developed for an Asian female, so I did get a lot of physical attention. They used to have games. They would walk by, just hit my boob. So I learned to fight then, too."

At home, Castrillon begged to go back to Canada. But it wasn't until she told a family friend about her male relative's behaviour that her request was taken seriously.

"I told him and he had this look on his face. It was so sad. That's when I think I realized that something bad had happened to me, because he just couldn't look me in the eye."

Shortly afterward, a plane ticket appeared and Castrillon was on her way to Canada and, she hoped, freedom. Instead, she was headed for the psych ward—and the street corners.

After just a few months in Canada, Castrillon admitted to a family doctor she felt sad and depressed. Another doctor prescribed antidepressants, which made her feel and behave oddly, she says. She began to make tiny incisions in her arm with an exacto blade. It's a disease called "self-mutilation" and Castrillon can still describe clearly the effect it had on her.

"It was self-abusive behaviour. I do not know where I got the idea, but it was such a release, almost meditative. It was so calming. It was something that was just mine. The ritual of it was almost like a moment of perfection."

Social workers at the school urged her to seek more intensive medical help. But once Castrillon checked herself into hospital, the doctors were not willing to let her walk out easily. The self-mutilation, for instance, had become "a serious addiction for me. It became very hard to kick." She'd also made a suicide attempt. She suddenly found herself classified as a mental health risk and barred from leaving the psychiatric ward. She panicked. And she was furious.

And more than a decade later, Castrillon is still angry about what she sees as medical treatment given to her against her will. "I couldn't say no to the pills. They made me like a zombie and I didn't like it."

She believes it was the medication, not mental illness, that produced her increasingly bizarre behaviour. "I was heavily medicated and restrained in the psych wards. The psychiatrists wouldn't listen to me."

Initially, doctors diagnosed depression, which Castrillon thinks was obvious, given her background and her circumstances. When that was changed to "borderline personality disorder," she scrounged up some psychiatric texts in the library. "They got pissed off that I was using their lingo. They'd say, 'Jaene, you're exhibiting attention-seeking behaviours,' and I'd say, 'Well, isn't that what borderlines do, Doc?' There were a lot of power struggles."

And a lot of drugs.

"They just said, 'You have panic attacks? Here's some Ativan. You're seeing aliens? Here's another pill. But now your depression's worse, so let's add some more pills. But you're manic, too. Here's another pill for that. But this combination isn't working. Let's swap this around.'"

For years she would labour under a variety of diagnoses: depression, manic depression, borderline personality disorder. One doctor pronounced her schizophrenic. Her childhood habit of talking to herself triggered more concern. Eventually, she would find doctors who were willing to involve her in decisions about her treatment, who even encouraged her to do her own research. But when her mother flew over from Hong Kong, mental health officials refused to release Castrillon into her care, worried she was "an unfit mother." Instead, Jaene was sent to a group home. She started back to school—and began to feel even more depressed.

Heavily medicated and suffering dramatic mood swings, Castrillon was forced to quit her job and turn to welfare, which also covered her $250 monthly drug bill.

When she couldn't pay her rent, she was evicted, and moved to the only place she could afford. It was a dank basement apartment with a padlock on the outside and mice and cockroaches inside; it flooded in the spring and she constantly hit her head on the furnace. "It just didn't help my depression."

Then the provincial government cut welfare payments to $520 from $690 per month, and ended coverage for certain drugs, including some of the ones Castrillon was taking. After paying $2 a pill for some medications and $450 in rent, she says she had little left for food, clothes or toiletries.

"You're really in a dead end. You can't get a job. You're medicated out of your mind. You're broke. You can barely afford soya sauce and rice after the rent. I couldn't go anywhere on the subway."

She was high all the time and sliding in and out of relationships with men who were also troubled. She'd become "promiscuous," so the shaky next step into prostitution was oddly short. It actually seemed like a viable idea.

"I was dating some older guy who would give me money and food and subway tokens. Some of my friends said, 'You can make money off of this.' It was better than dating some old guy who has control issues."

Not quite twenty, she began by placing an advertisement on a well-known telephone dating line, using popular code words: "Open-minded, voluptuous young Asian woman seeking generous gentleman."

And she got her first date: a man who paid her about the same for an hour's work as she received in two weeks on welfare. He also wanted it rough. Rather than feel exploited or demeaned—feelings that would awaken later—Castrillon says she felt relieved: she'd finally found a job she could manage. She could make a living. As for the violence, she agreed to it, having grown accustomed to being beaten long ago.

"I can go to the hospital and be crazy for two weeks and come back out, make a little money and survive on that," she recalls thinking.

Prostitution dovetailed heart-breakingly with Castrillon's mental illness. "Having issues with who I am? So, become a different person. Perfect! Disassociating, not connecting to other humans? Perfect! Having someone give me money instead of going on welfare? Even better," she says. "My pathologies were very useful all of a sudden.

"In the beginning it was a beautiful thing for me. I didn't have to get to know you. You weren't supposed to get to know the real me. I had a façade. Disassociation is very profitable in the sex trade."

She got something else with her new job, too—her first taste of power. "For a sliced-up, overweight, low self-esteem girl who really has no mainstream skills to make $160 to $250 an hour. Wooooh! Somebody's willing to pay $250 to spend an hour with me?"

At first, she felt a rush of control and a tremendous sense of relief. "There was that excitement, the fact that I was completely independent, that I could move from this hole in the ground. There were endless possibilities suddenly."

After years of poverty, the money meant a lot. "It wasn't a matter of looking at a CD and saying, 'That's not a choice for me to even buy because I'm on welfare.' It was, 'I like that CD but I'm *choosing* not to buy it, even though I could if I wanted to.' Mentally, it gave me a leg up to feel empowered, feel stronger."

Castrillon says prostitution also taught her something important about personal autonomy. "In the psych ward I didn't stick up for myself as much. I let people walk all over me to the point that I would suddenly blow up."

On the street, she had no choice but to assert herself. "You've got to set your boundaries and enforce them. It's training, and it sounds bad, but if a client doesn't respect your rules from the beginning, that client's going to turn out to be a bad date—tried, tested and true."

You've got to set your boundaries and enforce them.

Ironically, as Castrillon stood her ground with clients—something she'd never been able to do with her family or her doctors—her self-esteem grew. She withdrew, cold turkey, from the medication she took daily.

"A lot of people in the trade give their power away, whereas I realized, at the end of the day, I'm the one providing the service. So I am the one who owns the time. So if you're an ass, just because you paid me doesn't mean I have to put up with it."

In the later years on the street, as she grew bolder, Castrillon says she'd sometimes take a man's money and refuse to perform a service if he tried to hurt her or break one of her rules (such as never touching her neck—she didn't allow that because it was a sensation she actually found sensual).

"I used to just walk away with the money. I'd say, 'It's manners tax, because you don't have any manners.'"

Despite her burgeoning confidence, or perhaps because of it, Castrillon's perspective on working in "the trade" began to shift. She says she realized that, as much as she'd gained on the street, she had lost much more.

There was the fear, for instance, the constant fear of being hurt, raped, beaten or killed. One prostitute had disappeared; another was murdered. She remembers barely getting away with her own life after being cornered by a huge biker who'd just been released from prison after serving time for attempted murder.

And there was the constant humiliation.

"There are a lot of jerks out there and it was hard being constantly physically and emotionally abused. How many times can you hear that you're fat when you're buck naked? When a condom breaks, you totally freak out." Prostitution hurt her, she says. "All those little things that chip off your soul a little, through no fault of your own."

She never thought selling her body was easy, but she had believed for some time that "if I played the game right, like poker with the right hand, I could be okay."

But Castrillon was wrong.

"Everybody says that, but I have yet to meet a prostitute who's saved any amount of the money they've made. Most of them have transient lifestyles."

And while street life brings together some incredibly sensitive and talented people who've lost their way, it's also a magnet for those who want to harm others.

"The violence is phenomenal. There are a lot of not-very-nice guys in the world. In the trade, there were maybe one or two nice guys, but they were nice for a reason, because they wanted you to be their girlfriend and stop charging them," she says.

Be wary of anything that chips away at your soul.

Self-esteem asserts itself under unusual circumstances. As a prostitute Castrillon finally found a power she'd never known. But as her self-doubt eased, her tolerance for abuse decreased, as well.

"In the beginning I was so numb I didn't really care. That was my pathology, from the psych ward and the group home." But as her emotions surfaced, the young woman slowly realized how much she hated what she'd become. Escort agencies weren't hiring her, even though she was willing to do what other women wouldn't for customers, such as kissing, cuddling and anal sex. Even the sado-masochistic "dungeons" were saying no to her.

"I think I really snapped when I could no longer work indoors or in the dungeons. They want someone who is more profitable —young, preferably blonde."

To keep herself in the game in her early 20s, Castrillon says, she was forced to troll the street corners and offer extra, demeaning services—although she still refused to do anything, even perform oral sex, without a condom.

More emotionally awake than ever before, Castrillon was miserable. The harassment was awful. Passersby would swear and shout at her, try to run her over, throw things. "I broke every day. Every day you go out there, your heart's not in it and you're broken. You're trying to make ends meet. You just try to make money and survive the next day."

Increasingly, part of Castrillon was being drawn to something saner and smarter and safer. Rather than shun the agencies set up to help street kids, she made it part of her routine to drop by the counselling centres in downtown Toronto, listen and then float back to work. She got warm and got fed, but it was hard getting through to her: the independent little kid who fixed her own supper and put herself to bed at the age of six wasn't open to rescue.

Fortunately for Castrillon, there are people out there who don't give up. In many ways, that's why she's joined their ranks today. Night after night, counsellors would try to build her fragile ego. They told her what they saw: an articulate, compassionate and intelligent young woman.

"I'd say stupid things to my favourite counsellor like, 'You're paid to say that kind of stuff.' And she'd say, 'No, I'm paid to help you. I only say it because that's my opinion.' I'm still uncomfortable with compliments," Castrillon says, smiling though.

It took Castrillon six tries to leave her street job behind for good.

At one point, she enrolled in university, hoping to get a degree in Chinese literature, but she was still turning tricks at night and supporting her alcoholic boyfriend.

And then one day she had a painful epiphany when a couple in a car kept circling her, taking her photograph, threatening her. She called police for help. She told the officer she was afraid for her life. He forced her to admit she was a prostitute and then said,

'What do you want me to do about it?' That's when Castrillon concluded that as long as she sold sex, her job would define her as a person of little value. No one would see that she was a good person, who paid her taxes and would have excelled at university given the opportunity.

"I knew the truth was that as long as I was working as a prostitute, other people would see me for a 'ho' and never care about who I am. I realized I deserved a better life. I deserved to be respected and I deserved to be a person. Since that moment, my heart was never in the sex trade."

She enrolled in a street kids' project working with construction tools, and built a magnificent steel sculpture in a downtown Toronto neighbourhood. But she still wound up back in the trade. She was relieved to land a cashier's position, a so-called "straight" job that allowed her to pay the rent. But she lost it quickly when a patron recognized her as a prostitute.

And, honestly, she'd grown accustomed to the easy money, she says. "I am miserable making eight bucks an hour. So why wouldn't I go back to being miserable making 100 or 200 or 300 dollars an hour?"

Then, in 1998, another Toronto support group offered a free camping trip to its clients: five days of hiking and canoeing in the serenity of Algonquin Park. Just days before, Castrillon's exboyfriend had beaten her, but she blamed a bad client and downplayed the pain, afraid she'd be cut from the trip.

"I just toughed it out. I love nature. That kind of thing is very Zen for me. It was a free camping trip away from the trade for five days, not having to worry about money, rent, living in grungy hotels, stupid boyfriends."

It was late summer, the leaves lush, the air so fresh it lashes your lungs. And there was a semblance of family. "Eating granola with fresh-picked blueberries, campfires," she recalls, blissful still six years later.

There was a different type of pain—"a good pain"—from hiking hard and paddling and portaging the canoes, lifting them high overhead. "Ah!" she remembers. "I feel good today! I challenge myself!"

She was unreasonable in one respect. She wanted to see a moose, more, it seemed, than anything she'd ever wanted. A trip guide explained moose sightings weren't that common. The other campers, laughing and panting, teased her by announcing the arrival of "A moose!" with every snap of bush.

She remembers thinking, "I don't care. What kind of Canadian am I? I've never seen a moose. This would be a clearly defined Canadian moment for me."

For five days, nature held up and out, showing them loons, ducks, frogs, even a magnificent meteor shower one night. But no moose.

As the hikers paddled the last nine kilometres of their voyage, Castrillon accepted this disappointment like all the others. As usual, it was not going to happen for her.

Slowly she turned her head back to say goodbye—and there behind her, standing silently in a velvet green marsh, was a large female moose and her twin calves.

"I was freaking out! I think at that moment I said, 'Okay, who-ever's out there, or whatever's out there, you're giving me a hint. You're smiling at me. I can tell you're out there.' Not like a God figure, but there are some energies for me, enough that they gave me that experience."

To Castrillon, the gift of the moose meant this: "I wanted it bad enough that I got it. You couldn't have asked for anything bet-ter in life. That was the first epiphany."

Look for positive signs.

But this is not a fairy tale. After the trip, Castrillon went back to the trade, trying again and again to find a good job, being pushed back down by tricks and trouble—and a self-defeating attraction to bad boyfriends. She'd work a regular job during the day, and work the streets at night.

Then, lightning struck again—or so it seemed to Castrillon. In 1999, she was selected by community workers to participate in a Montreal conference that encouraged sexually exploited young people to tell their stories. "I was very lucky and honoured. I wanted to do right by my brothers and sisters, which I consider all people in the trade. I stayed with it. I was committed because I felt like all the things I complained about I had the ability to be part of the change now. I feel a sense of duty because I'm articulate enough."

From the start, Castrillon stood out; one meeting led to another, and eventually she found herself working with a handful of Toronto support agencies, and even the police. By 2001, she was administering a $120,000 youth advocacy program in Toronto. And now she is travelling the world as an outspoken reformer, determined to use her toughness to make things right for her "brothers and sisters." To do that, she has to stay positive herself.

"If you can't be optimistic for yourself, no one else owes it to you. No matter who you are, no matter how alone you feel, there is always someone going through something similar."

> *No matter how bad it gets,*
> *someone out there is sharing it.*

Now, after four years of sleeping on borrowed couches, she has a little apartment in Toronto, all her own, with appliances that work and an eclectic collection of pets: a white dove, an Asian dove, two cats, goldfish. "Funny what stable housing can do for your soul," she says.

"No one can truly say they don't matter in the world until they have lived their whole life. Get a pet and then you feel you matter, because without you, your pet will not live."

And the only people who get past her door these days are friends; she is working hard to build a sanctuary. "I love having my own place. I love coming home at night. My work is very heavy-duty. This is my sanctuary. Even if I have a bad day, if I want to cry, I'll grab my cat. It's my space; it's my control. Nobody can take that."

These days, she's crying more for other people than for herself. "I have a big heart. Being in the trade made me act tough but ultimately I am such a softie inside and I care. I just want to take people home and save them. I want to feed them all."

Castrillon's background makes it easier for her to understand kids working in the sex trade, but even she's shocked at what she finds. As a delegate to a Save the Children conference held in Nicaragua in 2002, she met children who lived and worked in a park, earning fifty cents to two dollars per client, for sex without condoms. The violence—the beatings, torture and burnings— was staggering, too.

"I just wanted to take them all home and say, 'There's a better life in the world.' Not being able to offer them something remotely resembling hope, what can you do? So you cry, you try your best to change the world, but you hang on to those memories because then you do your work. And your passion and commitment comes from honouring people."

Today, Castrillon's résumé is thick and impressive: working with a senator as co-chair of Health Canada's National Plan of Action on child sexual exploitation; collaborating with a police detective on an ambitious public education campaign; running her own social advocacy consulting firm. She's even thinking of going back to university. But right now, giving street kids a voice—the one she was denied for so long—is her highest priority.

"I cannot stand the idea of other people's suffering, that's why I help. I don't do it for karma or to feel better about myself. I do it because I have no choice, I can't bear thinking about all the horrible things that happen in the world every day and not do something about it."

If you know hell, do something to end it for others.

Castrillon is a work in progress. She stopped cutting herself when she found a place of her own and she's settled on a diagnosis: post-traumatic stress disorder, and manic depression. Ask her if she knows what event triggered her stress disorder, she says: "Yeah, my whole life."

At twenty-eight, she is now close to being the successful entrepreneur her mother always imagined. Still living back in Hong Kong, she has no idea what her daughter has endured. One day, mother and daughter will talk, Castrillon says.

"I think that when the time is right, I'll have to tell her. I don't want her to think it was her fault. That's a hard burden for a mother to carry. She's already had enough of her own burden."

Plus, there are other ways of putting your life back together, beyond blaming others. "When I was in Vancouver recently, [children's singer] Fred Penner was on stage singing a lullaby. I thought how I've never heard anybody sing me a lullaby and that made me cry.

"I'm the tough girl and I'm trying to hide it and this young person gives me a tissue and I'm so embarrassed. This is not my tough-girl mode!"

She stops and looks up, eyes clear and direct. "But you know, that's just life, right. Not everything's good. But things are good now, so that's all that matters."

Besides, there are other people in the world who can sing your lullabies, she says. "Fred Penner sang me mine."

It's never too late for someone to sing you a lullaby.

Instead of succumbing to self-pity, Castrillon looks back on her trials with some gratitude. "I look at all the challenges in terms of how they've given me the opportunity to grow, become a better person and learn certain extraordinary skills that otherwise I wouldn't have had.

"I would have just been somebody else going to school trying to figure out life. I wouldn't be someone who's twenty-eight, with a stable sense of self. I know where I want to go. I'm very happy in my career and my life and I make no compromises with who I am. I think that's an accomplishment and I don't think I would have had that without my past."

PASCAL RIBREAU

---

*A passionate French chef is paralyzed from
the waist down in a car crash but defies
those who say he'll never cook again.*

IT IS COLD IN UPTOWN TORONTO. Snowflakes eddy at the
blue lacquered door of Célestin, the chic restaurant on Mount
Pleasant Road. A slender woman in a little black dress offers
you a seat. Plump pockets of rabbit ravioli infused with shallots,
basil and olive oil swim in a big white bowl on your table. The chat-
ter of nearby diners, the warmth from the kitchen, the scent of
seared red pepper, butter and anise sauce envelop.

Through the open serving window you can see the cooks as
they whiz and whirl silently about their tasks. In the corner, near
the prep counter, there is a dark-haired boy-man with bright
eyes. Tom Cruise would play him in the movie. He is strapped into
a steel contraption that holds him erect and towering over his staff
—a charming, chopping, herb-waving mechanical man.

Pascal Ribreau pushes a button on his motorized, stand-up wheelchair and jets over to the fridge. He barely has time to glance out at the swelling crowd, but there is a tiny smile on his face. He is doing his two favourite things: cooking, and proving people wrong.

Did he feel suicidal when his doctor told him he would never walk again and that he must abandon his successful career as a chef?

"No! I ignored her."

Does he blame the driver, who, on a beautiful autumn afternoon, forced the car in which he was riding with his wife and friends off the road?

"No! Accidents are accidents. They happen. Let's say the driver made one mistake in his life and it turned into a crisis for me. We don't need more people to suffer from that. When I drove, maybe I wasn't perfect. I could have created a situation like that, too."

Did he succumb, as one easily might, to self-pity?

"No! When I ask, Why me? I say, Why not me? It could happen to anybody. If we had decided to wait two more minutes, the accident would not have happened, but then it happens to a lot of people every day."

Recovering from tragedy is far more complex, of course. But Ribreau is stubborn. Correction: *very* stubborn. It's a character trait that winds its way through his family tree, ruining relationships, estranging mothers and sons—but, ultimately, saving his life.

Ribreau was born in Paris, France, in 1969 to a family of restaurateurs whose most ardent hope was that he not follow in their weary, overworked footsteps. He saw little of his father, the owner of a couple of popular brasseries in the City of Light, who spent most days checking inventory and most nights "in the front of the house" tending to diners. His mother, too, spent long hours serving patrons in the family's restaurants.

The second of four children, Pascal was smart and obstinate —almost, he says, as difficult as his mother. Mme Ribreau and her son argued incessantly. She longed for him to leapfrog out of the service class into the professional offices of an architect. Clever at mathematics and very creative, Pascal liked the idea, but couldn't bear to live at home for the long years his studies would require. The more Pascal resisted his mother, the more irate she became.

In an uncanny foreshadowing, the family feuds made Pascal so ill he became immobilized at night, straitjacketed with anger in his bed. "I had a paralysis of the lower limbs during the night. The doctor said it was a nervous reaction to the stress. That didn't play very well with my mother."

So the difficult boy was sent not to a psychiatrist but, like Heidi, up into the mountains in Auvergne to stay with his grandparents for four "magnificent" months a year. The nervous affliction disappeared. Memories of that rustic retreat and the respect he earned from his maternal grandfather nurtured Ribreau, and he channelled his strong will into hard work. "He made me feel loved. He taught me about all that mattered in life."

His second paralysis would not be as easy to beat.

Ribreau's grandfather, Célestin Maury, was also "a man of strong ideas." The only son of a wealthy family, he had made the mistake of bringing home the wrong girl. His mother, especially, did not approve of the poor farmer's daughter. She gave Célestin a choice: find someone of a "better class" to marry or lose his inheritance. And so it was that Ribreau's grandfather, newly penniless, took his bride deep into the French countryside and built a solid stone house hauling the rocks for the foundation with his own hands. It was to this house that Ribreau was exiled each summer in the hope of easing the tension at home. But it was there that he found the love and dignity that would see him through the rest of his life.

If anything, those summer retreats made his city life more unbearable. And the feud between hot-tempered mother and son was unnerving his two younger brothers. "I didn't want them to suffer because I couldn't get along."

So, at fifteen, Ribreau ran away to cook. He knew it was the one thing sure to infuriate his mother, and it did. To this day they have very little to do with each other.

"It's the French way—dramatic at times," he says, his Parisian accent still strong. "But I couldn't live at home any more. There was no love or respect. Nothing I did was good enough. I was an adolescent at the time so that's probably part of it, too. I was a rebel."

Hell-bent on getting out and supporting himself, he had completed high school and cooking school, and now he nabbed a job as an apprentice at the Palais de Luxembourg in 1984. He was still so young he had to get special legal permission to take the post. Although cooking was a ticket out, it was hardly glamorous; as a neophyte, he spent long hours setting the stage for his masters—peeling, chopping and prepping ingredients. But Ribreau knew that a culinary diploma was a faster route to financial independence than academic studies. He wanted to be free—and he was willing to peel as many potatoes as it took.

Although his résumé would eventually read like a guide to France's best restaurants, it would be several years before he fell deeply in love with the craft.

For Ribreau, young and on his own, there was to be a beautiful woman in his story first. And as a young Canadian woman, Laurie Anderson, would learn, stubbornness in its more beautiful form is steadfastness.

In late summer 1987, Anderson was backpacking through Europe when she met a handsome, dark-haired boy in a Paris nightclub. They both remember the date: August 21. He could barely speak English; she barely spoke French. Yet they spent four happy days together before she continued her trip and returned to Canada. Three months later, unable to forget her French beau, Anderson flew back to Paris to spend six more weeks with him, and they decided they did not want to be apart again. After spending barely nine weeks together, they were married April 25 in Canada. They were both just nineteen years old. Sixteen years later—and counting—they are still together. "Obviously," Ribreau says, "there was a big attraction."

Together, they have seen triumph and tragedy, and there is no one either speaks more highly of than the other. "We grew up together. She is my best friend. I knew that before the accident, but once you go through something like this together, you know that person will always be there and I will, too."

It was in Toronto as a newlywed that Ribreau began to blossom into a man who one day could run his own restaurant. He won full-time positions at the prestigious Royal York Hotel and later the Sutton Place Hotel. He found a new mentor in the respected chef Niels Kjeldsen, from whom he learned a critical lesson: "Being a chef is about more than cooking. It is also about leading a team, inspiring people to work well and cook their best. Niels taught me how to do that."

In 1991, after Anderson graduated from fashion design in Toronto, they moved to Paris—what better city is there for food and fashion? Ribreau landed afterward at Les Roches, a famous three-star restaurant near sunny St. Tropez, presided over by the passionate and eccentric Laurent Tarridec. In exchange for exhausting hours and near-fanatical dedication, he showed Ribreau an exuberant approach to cooking, using fresh ingredients of the highest quality in ingenious combinations. It made up for the hysteria in the kitchen and the occasional knife flying past Ribreau's ear. But while there, Ribreau, who was not yet a Canadian citizen, was called up for his year of compulsory military service. What Anderson remembers about that year is not the time she spent alone, but what she glimpsed in her young husband.

"During Pascal's military service, which most French boys bitterly complain about and go to grudgingly, Pascal excelled in everything he was asked to do, from how to shoot a machine gun and launch a grenade to working in the officers' bar, where he kept his till straight while beating the officers at cards. He was awarded a medal of honour at the end of his service," she says.

Well trained, enthusiastic about the new cuisine that fused styles and nationalities, the young chef returned to Canada in 1993; the couple settled in Montreal to be close to Anderson's sister. They opened their first restaurant—Allumette—on rue Saint-Denis in the heart of romantic Montreal.

Ribreau loved the people, the Québécois culture—and he delighted in weaving a lighter, more modern twist into traditional French cuisine. Allumette went gold almost immediately, receiving flattering reviews from *The New York Times* and *The Washington Post*. At twenty-six, Ribreau was a culinary celebrity. For two years, his restaurant flourished, dishing up intense sauces and impeccable seafood; his rabbit ravioli was so popular he never managed to take it off the menu. And he drove himself hard, as always, working seven days a week, cooking two services a day, and running the business.

But in 1995 the threat of Quebec separatism, and then the tense aftermath of the failed independence referendum, drove out residents and crushed businesses. Lingering hostility floated in from the sidewalk.

Sometimes francophone patrons would refuse to sit at a certain table if there were anglophones sitting nearby. Ribreau and Anderson—the loving embodiment of bicultural, bilingual harmony—loathed the changed atmosphere and their faltering fortunes. The couple sold their restaurant and moved back to Toronto, where Ribreau quickly became the much doted-upon sous-chef at Provence, a pretty downtown restaurant.

And then everything changed.

On Thanksgiving weekend in 1999, Ribreau and Anderson went to Montreal to visit an old friend and his family. After an afternoon spent picking wild mushrooms, they ate a delicious picnic in the crisp fall air. Ribreau and his wife had tickets for a late afternoon flight back to Toronto. They wrapped up the last bits of cheese and crusty bread and climbed into the car. Ribreau's friend, Frédéric, was in the front and his wife, Valérie, took the wheel. Anderson and Ribreau sat in the back seat with two-year-old Samantha.

They had been driving along the quiet, two-lane country road for barely five minutes when a car in the oncoming lane tried to pass three vehicles in front of it. Its driver realized too late that he couldn't make it. Unable to steer back into his own lane, he was now hurtling straight for the car in which Ribreau and Anderson were riding.

Realizing they would be struck, Ribreau grabbed the child's car seat, shielding his goddaughter with his body. He held on tight.

To avoid being hit head-on, Valérie swung out of her lane, sending her car spinning on the gravel shoulder. And, then, in the split second before his world turned upside down, Ribreau looked up, straight into the panicked face of the other driver. Glass exploded. Metal screeched. Ribreau's car flipped over twice and he crashed through the rear window, flew up into the air and landed on his back. The car thundered down and stopped an inch from his feet.

"It is all clear, very clear. I don't have nightmares about it any more, but if I think about it, it's right there," he says, pointing to his forehead.

"I can see the car. I can see the face of the driver just beside me. It was a horror face."

Ribreau's back was broken, his spinal cord tattered and torn, either as he was propelled through the window or when he hit the ground. The little girl he had tried to shield escaped unharmed.

To this day, it is not that terrifying trip through the air or the "phenomenal pain" afterward that haunts Ribreau: it is what happened to his wife when she discovered the mangled body of her French love.

"One of the most troubling pictures in my life will always be the face of my wife holding my face. I was cut all over. I remember even the cops were throwing up because I looked so bad.

"But Laurie knew right away that something was terribly wrong. I told her I couldn't feel my body any more and I could see the distress in her face."

He also had a large open wound under his chin—"like another mouth"—and while others averted their eyes or were sick, Anderson tenderly held his face in her hands and waited for the ambulance.

It would take Ribreau himself considerably longer to truly confront his paralysis. "When the accident just happens, you don't understand the consequences. Not in the intensive care unit where the doctor says you will not walk; you will not feel your legs. Even there, you don't realize it because you're not active. You have drugs and friends and doctors around."

In an instant, a man of boundless energy became a "T8 incomplete paraplegic," with use of his arms alone. Two months in a morphine haze would pass before he was sufficiently recovered to fully appreciate that he was paralyzed. "And then you think, damn it, why can't I move my legs?"

Ribreau spent two weeks in the intensive care unit in Montreal, before being flown to Toronto's Sunnybrook Hospital. He was then moved to Lyndhurst Rehabilitation Centre, where for five months he would do stretching and weightlifting, and, eventually, spend hours strapped to a treadmill, exercising the legs he could not feel. Meanwhile, his arms had to learn to do the work of giants—hauling him from bed to wheelchair, pushing and pulling him to places his feet once carried him easily.

Yet, Ribreau is quick to point out that finally accepting the fact that he could not walk was a positive experience. "When you realize you've been paralyzed, you start doing more things. So it is counterbalancing." Physiotherapy. Wheelchair transfers. Exercise. Counselling.

Anderson recalls watching him struggle to regain what once were basic skills. A huge part of the training was simply relearning how to keep his balance, so that he could once again use a knife in the kitchen.

"There were no specific exercises or physiotherapy involved in preparing for the restaurant, more an attitude of 'just do it.' A less decisive person would have caved at many points when Pascal pushed ahead," she says.

And so Ribreau chose to see his new rehabilitation program not as the dreaded consequence of his accident, but as an accomplishment. "Maybe not in terms of mobility, but in terms of doing all the things you're supposed to do after the injury. So, you see every day you are regaining."

Ribreau used his willpower and his stubbornness to block the pain and the depression. He repeatedly assured his wife: "If I get depressed, I will not let it get me down."

Yet he admits that even with his fortitude, there was suffering and bouts of sadness. He remembers one day clearly. It was just before Christmas and he had won a ten-day release from the Lyndhurst Centre. Back at his old Toronto apartment, he was staring out the window at the beautiful park where he could no longer run, and at the tennis court where he would never again practise his serve. He ached with sadness. "All I could think of was what I wasn't able to do, how others would go on and I would be left." He admits he broke his promise: he was depressed and it was grinding him down.

But Ribreau quickly realized that free time was his enemy. Not only was it contrary to his normal schedule, it led to far too much idle thought. So he planned adventures and envisioned himself overcoming his physical limitations. His ambition drove some of his physicians mad, but setting goals created in him the expectation that he could reach them. That, in turn, freed his ambition and, ultimately, each accomplishment rebuilt his confidence. His formula: when they told him he couldn't do something, he set out to prove them wrong. "And I think it was my duty to show my wife that I was still the same person," he adds.

So, just ten weeks after the crippling crash, confined to a wheelchair and with his wounds barely healed, Ribreau invited a dozen friends and family for Christmas dinner and promised to cook the entire feast. Experts said it couldn't—and shouldn't—be done.

"But I wanted to cook! It was Christmas. I say: 'We're gonna have a great dinner; we're gonna drink great wine and party just like the old days.' And that's what we did."

It took Pascal two days to make that Christmas dinner. He stayed up into the early morning each day, clarifying stock, spinning out silken foie gras, julienning vegetables and, finally, roasting the succulent wild duck, a gift from a friend.

"I was exhausted. I was crazy. But I had to do it."

Is he stubborn?

"No!" He thinks for a moment. "Well, maybe in a good way."

Be stubborn—in a good way.

He paid for that burst of energy. After two days of cooking and celebrating, a sharp pain stabbed at his back, growing so fierce that he yelped as his wife struggled just to get him to his bed.

"This is so tough. This is so tough. This is so tough," he cried, he screamed, he moaned. He recalls repeating it at least twenty times. Years later, he's still a little embarrassed as he describes one of the few times he's permitted himself to slip into despair. But everything inside him—his stubbornness, his grandfather's tenacious example, his competitiveness, his love for his wife—won out. He willed himself through the pain and forced himself to push down the sadness.

How does he do it?

"Look, it's not my nature to be dark. I know a lot of people who just see the negative side. It's okay for a while. But then see what it brings into your life. It accentuates the burden you're already carrying. Let's make something positive out of it, instead."

Negativity will increase your burden: where
you had one problem, you now have two.

The suicide rate for those who suffer spinal injuries is high, Ribreau says. "It's such a dark path. I'm not judgmental because it is very tough. And depression sometimes is not a choice for people."

Before the accident, Ribreau had always taken a tough line on anyone who didn't push forward in life as fervently as he did. Now he was forced to re-examine that attitude.

"I have always been very hard on people who don't do enough with their life because there is only one opportunity. But with the spinal cord injury it's the burden of just every day. You have to face the reality every day. We wake up and half of our body is basically dead. So if you think about all those things every day, you can't go on. The burden is too heavy. So I focus on the things I want to achieve. Not what's behind me, but what I have to do."

Shortly after Ribreau's big dinner a doctor suggested he look for another profession, as cooking would now be too physically demanding. "But I'm good at that, not only at cooking but at directing people. That's what I do, that is my passion. I didn't want to find another job!"

So, Ribreau ignored the medical pessimists. "I didn't even bother arguing with them. This is your belief, but I know what I'm gonna do, so that's all. Don't let others decide what will happen to you as a result of your tragedy."

His accident has left him determined to help those who are also struggling. His eyes flash as he offers this warning: "Don't let others tell you what your outcome will be. No one knows you except *you*. Don't forget that!"

Don't let anybody decide what your outcome will be.

To cook again professionally, however, Ribreau knew he would have to stand—and do it for long periods. During his first week at Lyndhurst, he was thrilled to see a paraplegic with the same injury as his moving about with leg braces and a walker. He set this as a goal for himself and, after ten weeks in rehabilitation, he invited his wife to come visit him at lunch break. She found him standing on leg braces with a twinkly "What-do-you-think-of-your-husband-now?" look on his face. He wanted her to know he would do anything to please her, and would not abandon her to his disability.

Eventually, Ribreau rebuilt his endurance to the point where he could remain erect in a stand-up wheelchair for almost a full restaurant shift. But he had bigger dreams: if he was to become a bionic chef extraordinaire, he needed more ease of movement and more physical stability while cooking.

So he turned to engineers at Toronto's Motion Specialties to make it happen. It took more than a year to design and build the mobile standing-wheelchair prototype, which he found more flexible, more powerful and more comfortable than anything else that was on the market at the time. Although other stand-up chairs are available, he says his wheelchair is custom-built for every curve of his body; in it, he can zip around and switch from sitting to standing.

For weeks he pushed himself to stay standing longer and longer in the wheelchair until, despite a sore chest and swollen legs, he was able to remain erect for the dozen or so hours it took to maintain his kitchen mastery. Doctors and therapists, already worried by Ribreau's fierce determination and tendency to overdo, would have been shocked to learn what else he was plotting.

Although he loved working at Provence, the kitchen was not

fully equipped for a paraplegic chef. He thought: "Why not have my own place that I design to suit me perfectly?"

Rather than curtailing his ambition, Ribreau says, his accident forced him—or allowed him—to develop an even greater inner drive. That's the way he chooses to see it.

You are in charge of how you see your crisis.

"I don't ask myself *if* I can do it. I just ask myself *how* can I do it. If you put an 'if' in there, you're already putting an obstacle in front of yourself."

Asking whether you can do something adds an extra layer of analysis and doubt that must be overcome before the task itself can be attempted. It is a delaying mechanism, he says, often protecting you from the real fear of trying or failing or losing.

"Waste of time. Stop it," he advises.

Don't ask whether you can do it, ask how you can do it.

If you are determined enough, he says, you can emerge from tragedy with an even bigger appetite for risk, an even greater capacity for courage. Don't be surprised, he says, if friends and family have trouble keeping up. Even Ribreau's wife balked at some of his schemes—especially his decision to take a road trip to Montreal, doing all the driving himself. But he was on a mission that perhaps only he could fully understand. He knew the trip to Montreal would be both emotionally and physically taxing, but it was critical—for someone else's recovery. Although Ribreau wanted to regain his mobility for his own sake and his wife's sake, there was someone else suffering too—Valérie, the friend who was driving when the accident occurred and Ribreau was injured. He needed to give Valérie proof that she had not ruined his life, that he was moving beyond the ordeal.

"It was not her fault. She did the right thing. If she had not pulled off the road we all probably would have been killed. She saved our lives but I knew she felt terrible."

In 2001, as soon as he took possession of his new, specially equipped van—it had a ramp, hand controls and a swivel seat—he drove the four hours from Toronto to Montreal. Alone. Tired but triumphant, Ribreau pulled into Valérie's driveway and honked until she appeared, running toward him—crying.

"Oh, yes, she was shocked! I think it made her feel better to know that I felt better," he says.

And Ribreau just kept pushing, physically testing himself as never before, and in so doing sending a message to anyone feeling defeated by disability or accident. Less than a year after his accident, Ribreau was inspired by a man named Charlie Cetinski, who after having been paralyzed in a plane crash organized a wheelchair marathon to raise money for a new rehab centre in Hamilton. Ribreau knew how hard his life would have been without the Lyndhurst facility in Toronto; he offered to help Cetinski raise money. Besides, Ribreau has a big problem saying no to a challenge.

"I decide I am going to try the marathon, in a wheelchair. It is going to take me a very long time to get in shape for this. But if I do it, well what can I not do?"

For eight months he sweated, ached and trained with some of Canada's best wheelchair athletes, lifting weights, wheeling mile after mile, and building his mental stamina as well. In June 2001, he was one of six participants in the Golden Horseshoe Marathon, wheeling for five days from Niagara Falls to Toronto. There were seemingly endless highway stretches, steep hills and tough weather. And while safety vans accompanied them on the trek, Ribreau wanted to do it all by himself.

On each of the five days, the racers had to complete one full marathon of forty-two kilometres. It was not until the third day, though, that Ribreau began to think he'd finally been beaten.

Just three kilometres short of the day's finish line, he found his strength failing. He was more tired than he'd ever been in his life, and his arms seemed to melt from their sockets. "I was just exhausted, and my vision was blurred. I really didn't know if I could make it."

But as he sat at the bottom of that steep hill in Hamilton, bathed in sweat, thinking about failure and what it would mean to the rest of his life, Pascal Ribreau looked up and saw the impossible. His beloved grandfather was at the top of the road, beckoning.

And he suddenly remembered his youthful summer visits to the French mountains, where he and the old man who loved him so fiercely had chopped and stripped birch trees together, wrapped them with chains, and hauled them up the hills.

"And then suddenly, I saw my grandfather pulling me, like the wood, all the way up the hill."

Arms grinding, neck and shoulders straining forward, Ribreau broke the back of that hill and made it all the way to the top.

"I finished with someone pulling me. I am not superstitious. I am not religious, but that marked me," Ribreau says, and there are tears as he remembers.

Célestin Maury had passed away one year earlier.

To this day, his grandfather is his hero and his role model. As a tribute to him, he named his popular Toronto restaurant "Célestin," and threw open its doors on New Year's Eve, December 31, 2002.

When depression or despair does sneak up on him, Ribreau reminds himself that everyone carries burdens in this life. It's not what you deal with, but how.

"When I think of how he built his house and carved his own stone, raised nine children and fought in the Second World War, it puts things in perspective. Choose the path. My grandfather chose his wife, whom he loved, instead of choosing his mother, who had money. That was his integrity, his dignity."

It's not what you deal with, but how.

Ribreau is once again a big name in the restaurant business, but now he's got another calling as well: role model. Célestin is a meeting place for the disabled, and his career is an inspiration to anyone facing monumental challenge.

"If I can share what my grandfather was able to give me and I give it to others, it's a cure for me, too. You know? When I make progress and I help other people to make progress, then it makes me feel better."

And so, as it turns out, the stubbornness that ruined relationships and drove teachers to distraction is Ribreau's salvation.

And he wants more. "Look, I'm not a dreamer, but I think I should tell you that I do want to walk. I do plan to walk again."

* * *

A Gift from Pascal

A reviewer once said that Pascal Ribreau created "poetry on a plate." Here's a recipe that will always remind the chef of that critical Christmas, shortly after his paralyzing accident, when he decided to take his fate into his own hands.

DUCK CONFIT AND FOIE GRAS TORTE
WITH SAVOY CABBAGE

- 2 large Savoy cabbage
- 2 confit duck legs (can be homemade or purchased)
  500 g foie gras
- 12 very thin slices of double-smoked bacon
- 2 sheets of puff pastry (3mm thick)
- 3 tablespoons butter
- 1 egg yolk
  salt and pepper to taste

Preheat oven to 375°

1. Cut off cabbage stem and break off leaves. Cook leaves in boiling water until tender (about three minutes).
2. Dry leaves and then sauté them in butter. Set aside to let cool.
3. Remove all meat from duck leg confit and separate by hand into small pieces.
4. Slice foie gras lengthwise into four pieces and pan sear both sides of each piece. Set aside to cool.
5. Once all ingredients have cooled, cut one puff pastry sheet into an eight-inch round, cut the other to twelve-inches.
6. Place the eight-inch puff pastry round on a baking sheet and layer the ingredients in the following order: half of all cabbage leaves, duck, bacon, foie gras. Season with salt and pepper on each layer.
7. Cover with the remaining cabbage leaves and then the second puff pastry sheet. Pinch and score edges.
8. Brush top with egg yolk.

Place in the middle rack in the oven and bake for twenty minutes.

Ribreau served this dish to his astonished friends with oven-roasted wild duck and roasted Italian chestnuts with a red wine cassis sauce on the side.

———————

Here is another recipe, which Ribreau created for his new Toronto restaurant, Célestin, and his new life, post-paralysis—a dish, a restaurant and a future that doubters thought could never be.

ROASTED EGGPLANT TERRINE WITH
GOAT CHEESE AND FRESH HERBS

½ pint each of red and golden cherry tomatoes
1 large eggplant
1 pound goat cheese
3 gelatine leaves
2 tablespoons 35 percent cream
3 tablespoons olive oil
3 tablespoons each chopped basil, parsley and marjoram
3 tablespoons balsamic vinegar
½ cup baby arugula
4 tablespoons of chopped shallots
  Salt and pepper to taste
1 terrine mould

1. Wash and slice eggplant lengthwise into 3mm slices (can use mandolin).
2. Heat olive oil in a saucepan and cook eggplant slices until golden brown (about thirty seconds each side).
3. Place slices on paper towel to absorb excess olive oil.
4. Place gelatine leaves in a bowl of cold water.
5. Beat goat cheese in a food processor until light and fluffy.
6. Heat two tablespoons cream in saucepan over medium heat.
7. Remove gelatine leaves from water bath by hand and squeeze out excess water. Place in heated cream until it dissolves (about ten seconds).
8. Pour cream mixture over goat cheese and mix with a spatula.
9. Sprinkle eggplant with salt and place slices to line the terrine mould with ends folding over edges to the outside. Fill with cheese mixture.
10. Sprinkle with chopped herbs.

11. Close eggplant ends over cheese filling and cover terrine with plastic wrap.
12. Place in the fridge and let sit for two hours.
13. Cut cherry tomatoes in half and toss with balsamic vinegar, chopped herbs and shallots.
14. Remove terrine from mould and cut slices approximately 1 cm thick.
15. Place two slices on plate and garnish with cherry tomatoes and baby arugula. Drizzle with olive oil.

Finally, here is Ribreau's much-loved rabbit ravioli, a dish he made before and after the accident, a symbol of life's continuity.

RABBIT RAVIOLI

1 small rabbit (about 2 lb.) cut into pieces
1 package of wonton wrappers
1 cup of white wine and four cups of water
1 small onion, diced
1 carrot, diced
1 head of garlic cut in half
2 tablespoons of balsamic vinegar
2 bunches of fresh basil
1 bunch of parsley
1 cup of olive oil
4 ounces of parmesan shavings
½ cup pitted Niçoise black olives
½ cup toasted pine nuts
  salt and pepper

Serves 10

Sear the rabbit on both sides, then add the vegetables and the *stems* of the fresh herbs, deglaze with the wine and reduce for one minute before adding the water. Add garlic and let the rabbit simmer for two hours until the meat is tender, then let it cool down.

Wash half of the fresh herbs and cook them for fifteen seconds in boiling salted water and cool them in a bowl of ice water. Put the olive oil in a blender and mix these herbs with it and reserve.

Remove all the meat from the rabbit, shred it with a fork and season it with the rest of the fresh herbs, chopped and with some olive oil. Add the balsamic vinegar. Add salt and pepper to taste.

Stuff all of the ravioli dough with the rabbit meat and set aside.

To serve: Cook the ravioli for two minutes in salted boiling water, then put them in the rabbit stock to finish cooking for another two minutes. Garnish a bowl for each person with the olive oil and herb paste. Add five ravioli garnished with pitted black olives, pine nuts and the parmesan shavings.

ISOBEL ANDERSON

---

*A police officer faces death in the
Rhodesian civil war, and at the tip of
a hypodermic needle in Canada, before
learning she's not afraid to die.*

INTERVIEWING Sergeant Isobel Anderson is unnerving. In many ways, a policewoman is in the same business as a journalist—the art of observation. We talk for hours in her modest Ottawa living room and again later in her car, and she rarely takes her eyes—or her senses—off me, even when she is driving.

It's the closest I can recall being watched on the job. I figure Anderson must be a very good cop.

Yet she looks nothing like a veteran of two police forces, Canadian and Rhodesian—or at least, nothing like the tough stereotype. Short, petite even, with a tender, tentative smile and an unthreatening presence.

Come closer though, spend more time with her, and you can sense a power, like a yo-yo wound tight and ready to fly. And if you push against her—asking tough questions or debating her conclusions, she's unflappable, immovable: it's like nudging at a cement wall.

When she applied to the Ottawa Police Service, friends warned her she would never be hired. She was thirty-five years old, an immigrant who spoke with an accent, and had no university degree.

"I refused to believe that, even though only thirty applications would be selected out of about two thousand. I focused on the goal, and was hired. I always look at obstacles and hurdles as opportunities to excel."

Now friends know better than to discourage her drive. Watching Anderson in action as she tried to change police management's mind about yet another policy, a fellow officer said, "Hasn't it hit them yet that every time they tell you that you can't do something, you go above and beyond what you need to do to achieve it, even beyond their expectations of you?"

She's lived through civil war, wrestled armed thieves to the ground, captured a pedophile, and soldiered on in the face of racial segregation.

But in many ways, her story of courage is about the tiny tip of a hypodermic needle, and the injury that could have ended her career and taken her life.

Isobel Granger was born in 1958 in a country of white minority rule called Rhodesia (since renamed Zimbabwe). She grew up in Bulawayo's "coloured" neighbourhood, sandwiched between the white-skinned elite and the black underclass, whose skin was darker than her own. Officially, she was classified as a "coloured" and therefore banned from taking anything from a white person, whether that was a job or a seat on the bus.

Unofficially, Anderson's heritage is more complicated. In the late 1800s, a white British prospector went to South Africa in search of gold; he also found a black female companion. The black woman was Anderson's great-grandmother. She moved into a small house in the shadow of the white prospector's big house and bore him a son of "mixed birth." That son, Anderson's grandfather, also chose a wife of "mixed birth" who was so fair she often passed as white. The night she gave birth to her son, however, officially marked her tumble down the funnel of segregation. Deep in labour, Anderson's fair-skinned grandmother was rushed to the hospital in Bulawayo's "white area," where she gave birth to Anderson's father.

But alarm ensued when the little boy with kinky black hair slid from his pale mother. As the family story is told and retold—oh, how many times Anderson, growing up, heard the parable of racism—mother and baby somehow "disappeared" from the hospital in the middle of the night. It was incomprehensible that a baby with obvious black genes could be permitted to stay, so they were whisked away to a "coloured" hospital. "That's how I grew up. Those are our family stories," Anderson says.

Despite her "middlin'" status—part white and part black—it was the dark pigment in Anderson's lineage that defined and imprisoned her Rhodesian youth. At home, her parents were staunchly egalitarian, teaching their children that segregation was wrong and nurturing their self-esteem. But out in the community, the spirited tomboy was forbidden to walk on the sidewalks or fraternize with whites.

In the early 1970s, she narrowly escaped arrest when she refused to give up her bus seat to a white girl. Outraged, the white driver threatened to call the police; Anderson, just thirteen, hopped off the bus and flew the seven miles home, sweating and nervous. "The police were absolutely feared. When you saw them coming to your house, you knew they weren't going to be friendly."

Her country's obsession with skin pigment pervaded every aspect of her life. While her school was not integrated with the white community, staff and students still enforced a hierarchy based on degrees of skin colour; the darker the skin, the lower the status.

Anderson has a beautiful singing voice, and as a child was frequently invited to entertain at church and at school; she was so admired that she never needed to audition. It was natural she'd be chosen for the starring role of "princess" in the big school play. She was elated, until a teacher led her backstage and ordered her to stand concealed behind the curtain during the performance. Before the audience, onstage, a lighter-skinned girl acted the role, mouthing the songs Anderson was singing backstage and out of sight. "I didn't understand because I just enjoyed singing so much," she recalls.

But another one of the teachers understood, and she was furious. "I remember her shaking me after that and saying to me, 'Don't you ever let anybody put you behind the curtain again.'" That teacher complained to the headmaster, announcing, "If she's good enough to sing, she's good enough to stand *onstage* and sing." It was the same message her parents conveyed at home. "My mother and father always taught us that there's nobody else that's better than you and that you're not better than anybody else. You treat everybody equally, and don't ever let anybody tell you that you're not good enough."

> *There is nobody else better than you, and*
> *you are not better than anyone else.*

Reading the newspaper one day, an eighteen-year-old Anderson saw an advertisement urging people who wanted a career that "makes a difference" to join the Rhodesian national police force. A good-looking police officer was pictured in his crisp uniform.

Another "coloured girl" might have thrown away the paper. Another girl might have worked anywhere else rather than join forces with the enemy. But Isobel Anderson is entirely different.

"I have always believed that in order to effect change, you have to jump right in, as scary as it is sometimes."

Anderson knew that her surname—Granger—sounded English, and that if she used the address of her father's employer in the white district, police officials would likely err and consider her application, at least until they caught sight of her. She admits that part of her craved the shock impact. But in many ways, the rebel in her was already looking for work outside the limits imposed on her by her skin colour and gender.

"The Rhodesian police force—although living in Rhodesia, which was predominantly black—had preconceived ideas about blacks. Most of them did not see us as equals and I knew that the best way to change the attitudes of the misinformed is through education. Once they worked with me, and others like me, I thought they'd realize that the main difference between us was pigmentation. Every other difference could be attributed to privileges or lack of privileges such as schooling," she says.

And another thing: "I felt I had the right to be there."

She got the interview, and had the effect she wanted. The chief inspector was certainly "taken aback" when he saw her, she remembers. "You know we don't hire coloured people. Why have you applied?" he asked.

What Anderson *heard* was not just rejection, but a challenge to her equality—the one right that she knew she was entitled to, as she had been taught by her brave grade-school teacher and her parents. She straightened up, and proceeded to list her attributes. "I don't see what there is that a white girl can do that I can't do. I think I'd make a very good police officer." He didn't reply.

Anderson was dismissed and forgot about joining the force. But to her surprise, she was called back for psychological and aptitude testing, and then asked to present herself to the police board for an interview. Insincere political correctness was one thing, she recalls thinking, "but this is going a little too far."

Anderson, it turned out, had scored very high on the physical and mental agility tests. But she also thinks the force knew the world was watching, and beginning to ask questions about segregation. "So the force was being politically correct, not only toward blacks but toward women in policing, too. Despite the fact that I came from an underprivileged part of that society, I was well educated and physically fit. I challenged them to turn me down."

In 1978, she became the first black female police officer to be hired in Rhodesia, and the first non-white person of either sex to join the elite ranks of patrol officers.

That's when the real trouble began.

Night shift. The downtown Bulawayo officers' mess. Anderson walked into the packed cafeteria and stopped as, one by one, her fellow officers sneered and narrowed their eyes. A male officer stands. "We're forced to work with you now, but I don't think we should be subjected to eating with you," he announced.

Inside, Anderson says, she was "shaking like a leaf," but she'd never had much tolerance for condescension, so she sucked in some air and looked him in the eye. "As far as I know, I am a patrol officer. I scored one of the top marks in my class. If you think that you don't want to eat with me, then feel free to leave any time, but I am staying."

Anderson marched to the food lineup and stuck out her tray. The nervous black cashier was afraid to serve her. She stood, she waited. Some of the officers threw their food into the garbage bin and swept past her. Slowly, though, the buzz of quiet conversation resumed, and Anderson got her bacon and eggs. She'd held her ground.

She had come well prepared for the prejudice. Her white female comrades at police college had been even more blatantly racist, she says, refusing to use any shower or toilet she'd touched.

One afternoon, a group of police recruits had circled Anderson in their dormitory. The women stood in a tight circle until one of them spoke up: "I do not think that we should be subjected to sharing living quarters, let alone working side by side with you. You have not even completed the evolutionary process yet."

Inside, Anderson admits, she was thinking, "What am I doing here?" She was angry, embarrassed and hurt. Rather than flee, though, and let the small minds win, she negotiated a deal with the women: if they designated one toilet and one shower just for the "coloured girl," she would promise not to go near the rest of the facilities.

Today, looking around her spotless Ottawa apartment, it's easy to guess the outcome. "My kitchen and the washrooms are places that I like to have especially clean all the time. My mum was like that and I ride my girls when they're messy." By the end of her police training, the women had stopped shunning Anderson— and were using her spotless bathroom rather than their own.

But why bother? Why not quit, run, fall into a deep depression, or—at least—find a less combative job? Like so many people who survive and even seem to thrive on adversity, Anderson had had an epiphany. In a train station.

She was nineteen years old, about to leave her hometown to embark on her police training. As she climbed the dusty steps of the passenger car, she turned to take a last look around. Walking and running toward her from every corner of the station were friends, colleagues, family members and former teachers. "Half my community is there at the railway station and they're telling me that what I do when I get to police college will impact on all of them," she remembers.

The teenager balked. "I just want to be a police officer. I'm just a kid and now I have this responsibility on my shoulders?" But later when she was confronted by colleagues who wouldn't eat with her, live with her or allow her to use the toilet, Anderson suddenly understood the yearning and the hope she'd seen on her neighbours' faces. And she made a choice. She chose not to disappoint them.

"Some people say that I'm superstitious. I do believe that people have roles that they have to play. I think you are chosen, slated, for that role and you just play it to the best of your ability."

**If you are chosen for a role in life,
play it to the best of your ability.**

When faced with hardship, we may feel that all has perished, all has been taken from us. But in any situation, there is always one thing remaining, she says.

And that something is choice.

"I believe that whatever happens to you, you always have choices. You have the choice to react negatively or to react positively. I believe that when someone does something to you, if you take a split second to think about the consequences of your reaction to their action, 99 percent of the time you won't do what you set out to do in the beginning."

Anderson admits she considered violence, lashing out at those who harassed and intimidated her throughout her life. Four of her brothers belonged to the military and she'd spent her days running, climbing and hunting with them. Although she's always had "a healthy respect" for guns and force, she knew how to hurt people, and she was strong. But she refused to let herself succumb, to let her persecutors put her where they wanted her: in the wrong, and therefore vulnerable. Instead, she decided that it is always better to explode a prejudice.

It is always better to educate than to retaliate.

Helping to change attitudes, it turns out, was the easier task. In 1979, the newly minted police officer Isobel Anderson walked straight into the bloody war that had been raging for years between Rhodesia's white regime and black guerrilla factions.

One day, Anderson was learning how to set up a roadblock. "I remember the instructor saying if you heard him say *Hit the deck*, you should just go down and fire back at wherever shots are coming from. I'm thinking, 'Oh my God, what the heck am I doing here?' We actually were being fired upon. But from there, I never looked back. I grew up and I became old overnight."

One evening she found it hard to sleep with what sounded like a constant rapping at her door. In the morning, she joined the police crews picking up the corpses; the rapping had been gunfire. The civil war had begun in earnest.

"For three days, all we did was pick up bodies. I remember delivering a child. This lady was almost full term and she had a big piece of shrapnel sticking out of her tummy. She said, 'Is my baby okay?' but I didn't know anything about babies."

Anderson comforted her, delivered the baby and watched as the new mother was driven to the hospital in the back of a pick-up truck, perched on a pile of corpses.

"The fighting was so bad. You just did what you could do. I lost some friends. But when you look back at it now, it doesn't seem real."

People were dying so quickly and in such huge numbers that the women in her family were each assigned "funeral days" during the week. On Tuesday, Anderson would represent the family at all the burials; on Wednesday her sister would go; Thursday, her mother. "Every night at eight o'clock we'd listen to the radio and they'd announce the people who died on that day. We'd support each other but death was very much a part of our lives."

Eventually, Anderson woke and realized her first thought was not *whether* anyone would be killed that day, but how *many* would die. "I remember thinking that it's not good to be expecting that as part of your normal life. So I decided it was time to quit."

She doubts she will ever want to talk in detail about the killing, whether she might have been responsible for taking human life during the uprisings. "I've been involved in a lot of shootings. But lots of times we'd go to places where we'd get involved in gunfights. A lot of times we wouldn't find out whose bullet actually caused the fatality."

In 1980, Zimbabwe gained independence and Anderson married; she had her first baby, a son, in 1982 and went back to policing. By now, her country was a violent political stew of mass murders and arson as leaders of the triumphant black factions turned on each other.

Being neither white nor black in a society that still defined itself along race lines—albeit with the power relationship reversed—was too wearying and too frightening. At one point, she was ordered to patrol her own "coloured" neighbourhood; it was an assignment that put her, she says, in an untenable position.

So, by the time Anderson left the police force and took an accounting job in an all-white company, she knew how to handle the prejudice. She reported for work early the first day, but none of the white women would let her into the office; she was the first "coloured" person ever hired. Her boss arrived later and unlocked the door for her, but the women congregated at the end of the office and talked in loud voices about how "the standards are falling." Quickly, they floated rumours that she was stealing office supplies, including toilet paper from the company washroom.

Again, Anderson toughed it out. "I said to the one lady, 'Actually, my husband works for a paper packaging place and we get only the best toilet paper. I am willing to bring in a box every now and again, because we only use the good stuff at home.'" It was a good story with the added advantage of being true. A couple of years later, when one of Anderson's chief antagonists was emigrating, the woman apologized. "I've never lived with black people. I never, ever communicated with them, never socialized. I'm sorry I treated you so badly."

Anderson accepted the apology swiftly. "No, that's fine," she said. "As long as wherever you go now, maybe when you see another black person, maybe you can think about what happened to me."

The problem with holding grudges, Anderson says, is that they get heavy. "I would not want to have a chip on my shoulder because I have small shoulders and there are just going to be too many of them."

In the bleakest moments, she heard her mother's counsel again and again. "Just put your head up and don't let anybody tell you that they're better than you because they are not." Not put your head *down*, as we hear so often, but up. You take a lot more in your face at that altitude, but you see and taste and experience so much more, too.

To win, don't put your head down—lift it up.

She'd always dreamed of Canada, and now with three children, she longed for a country where race didn't divide and destroy. Although segregation had officially ended, she knew it would take years before the society would really change. When her husband was offered a job in Ottawa, they emigrated in 1989. Anderson stayed home to raise their three kids, just two, four and six at the time, while babysitting other children, too.

In 1992, in need of money and pining for the profession she loved, Anderson submitted her application to the Ottawa police force but abandoned it when her husband protested. He wanted her to have a more traditional job; fissures in their relationship were widening. She tried contract clerical work but found it neither steady nor challenging enough.

It was time to face the truth about herself—even if it threatened the familiar security of her marriage. "I wanted to be back policing. It's what I love. If it wasn't for what happened in Zimbabwe, I would still be a police officer," she recalls thinking.

In 1994, she telephoned the Ottawa police department again, and this time reached a woman who was stunned to hear from her, because she had just earlier that day looked at Anderson's two-year-old application, and wished the experienced officer hadn't backed out. "She said, 'I am so glad you called. Come on in.' Before I knew it, I was given my uniforms and I'd done all my tests."

But women were still a minority on the Ottawa force, and as for black female officers, there weren't any. Anderson was one of the first five to be hired. Here she was, breaking new ground—again.

"A lot of people there had never worked with minorities. I remember being told by people to be careful because some of the older guys are set in their ways. But the amazing thing is that those guys became some of my best friends."

Police college wasn't entirely welcoming. The female driving instructor asked her on the first day how she expected to drive in Canada when she was accustomed to using the other side of the road in Africa. That officer's harassment grew so obvious, Anderson says, that other colleagues, many of them kind and supportive, urged her to complain. And while the top brass reassured her that she'd be given an independent driving test, her self-confidence was shaken. "It does affect you when someone tells you that you can't do something, and knowing I was driving my children around, I began to wonder whether I was endangering them."

What Anderson didn't volunteer at the time was that in Zimbabwe she had deftly driven a police cruiser, an armoured personnel carrier during the war and an escort car in the prime minister's motorcade. So did she know how to drive? "Oh, yes, I wouldn't be alive if I didn't."

Eventually, Sue O'Sullivan, a senior officer at the time, arranged for an independent instructor to test Anderson. He passed her with high grades. "I believe things happen for a reason," she says. "At every time in my life where I've gone through difficulty, there's always been somebody that's been placed there, just like a mentor. Sue O'Sullivan just stood behind me."

Facing conflict over and over can leave us despondent, bitter and angry, or, as Anderson says, it can make us smarter and stronger.

"I don't think that anger has any place in the workplace. It impairs judgment and alienates people. But I do not run from confrontation. I listen and paraphrase to show I understand, even when what they are saying doesn't sound right to me!"

That willingness to compromise, coupled with a positive attitude—always giving people the benefit of the doubt, especially in a disagreement—has helped Anderson push through more serious challenges than many of us will ever battle.

"I try to create a positive environment at work. Stay away from gossip. If it is not positive, do not say it. And don't give up. If I don't get no for an answer, then I know that it is not a closed door. Maybe I just have to work harder."

If you don't get no for an answer, the door's still open.

Yet, looking back, Anderson says so much of what she endured was just a dress rehearsal for the real fight of her life.

In June 1997, after suffering a year of excruciating back pain, Anderson was diagnosed with a tumour on the base of her spine. Risky surgery was scheduled for November and the mother of three knew she'd be unable to work for months. Her marriage, already strained by her non-traditional career, was shuddering to its end under the weight of financial pressures and, now, her illness.

In October, just a month before her scheduled surgery, Anderson was sitting alone in her cruiser in downtown Ottawa when she got a call about an armed robbery in progress. She glanced up, realized she was within a block of the pharmacy that had just been held up, and sped to the address. Dashing inside, she comforted distraught customers, called an ambulance, and then hopped back into her car, taking a witness along to help her track down the bandit. Following her uncanny instincts, she zipped down some side streets and pulled up right beside the scruffy suspect.

Warned by dispatch that he was carrying a gun, Anderson performed a single-handed "high risk" arrest and handcuffed him. Before searching him, she asked him three times: "Do you have anything that could harm you or harm me—a knife, a needle, a gun?" Three times he said no.

So, Anderson patted him down, then reached in to pull out his pants pocket and immediately felt a fierce stab. Quickly, she pulled her hand away, and discovered a hypodermic needle plunged so deeply into her palm it was still hanging there.

In that terrifying split second, she also saw her death sentence: swirls of red blood in the needle's cartridge. She panicked, and imagined the worst. "I have a tumour. I want to have an operation, now I have AIDS? What about my children? My husband had just been laid off. I was the sole breadwinner. I want to see my children graduate! I want to see them go to university! I want to see them get married! All those things you normally wouldn't think of flash through your head."

To make matters worse, there were few supports in place for police officers injured this way in the line of duty: once other officers arrived to take over the arrest, she was expected to drive herself to the hospital and handle the shock alone.

Yet according to the emergency room doctor, she had less than two hours to make a life-or-death decision. At the time, that was the tiny window of opportunity for someone who'd been exposed to the HIV-AIDS virus to receive a special serum, a drug "cocktail" including the antiretroviral drug AZT that had the potential to reduce or even eliminate the risk of contracting the full-blown disease.

Unfortunately, it was a gamble. Testing her for HIV would take much longer than two hours, but if she waited, she would miss any opportunity of nailing the illness.

Of course, making the decision to take the drugs before she

knew whether she needed them was just the beginning of the ordeal. Taking the cocktail could certainly result in powerful side effects; not taking it could result in death.

To help, the doctor suggested they also test the man Anderson had arrested to see whether he tested positive for HIV or hepatitis C. She'd already been vaccinated against hepatitis B.

She agreed, and then got another shock. Although the suspect had potentially put her life in jeopardy by lying to her about the needle in his pocket, no one could compel him to submit to a blood test. His legal rights trumped her health concerns.

"He robbed a place, and look what he did to all those people and to me. I have to know if I have something in my body that is going to affect me. I have a responsibility to my family, plus the people I work with, but he's not compellable."

Anderson took the powerful cocktail and began to feel ill immediately. When she arrived back at the police station, another officer told her the assailant, who was later convicted of armed robbery, had finally agreed to take the blood test—in exchange for a hamburger from a fast food restaurant.

More than three days later—and hours and hours of fatigue and vomiting for Anderson—the suspect's AIDS test came back negative. She was able to cut short the 30-day drug treatment and went back to work. But the strain of the ordeal left its mark.

Over the next few weeks Anderson would feel physically ravaged. Almost half of her hair, which she'd always considered one of her most attractive physical attributes, fell out. She broke out in hives. And although there was no risk of AIDS, it turned out the stick-up man did have hepatitis C. It took Anderson more than a year of tests to determine for certain that she hadn't contracted the illness.

Although relieved, Anderson says she also felt guilty. She recalled that when one of her colleagues had been stabbed by a suspect's needle, she'd been sympathetic, but not supportive enough. "In a shooting, everybody is all over you. Either it is fatal or you have this wound, this injury, and it's dealt with immediately." But coming into contact with an unknowable—a disease or a substance that could take years to hurt you—was different. "People can't put their finger on it as easily, yet it's the emotional trauma that is probably the worst thing."

So, rather than walk away once she'd received a clean bill of health, Anderson swung into action. "We're here for a reason. I feel that I am supposed to try, every day, to make this a better place to be."

Each of us is here for a reason.

Doing something to make conditions better for police officers helped restore her sense of control, and mitigated the sense of futility that can follow a harrowing experience.

For five years she lobbied senior police officials and members of the government, and in the end she prevailed; the law would be changed. She hadn't hesitated to throw her weight up against Canada's constitution, and face down opposition from some members of the HIV support community: not an easy task for a woman who hadn't been to university, let alone law school. She did what she believed made sense and was morally correct.

"I believe the Charter of Rights and Freedoms was intended to balance our rights, so I argued that if anyone, including me, exposes someone else to bodily fluids, their right to privacy should not outweigh the other person's right to health and safety."

When some members of the gay community argued that such a law would feed the stereotypes about homosexuality and disease, Anderson challenged *them* to stop casting aspersions on their own. "I told them that AIDS is not a gay disease and people are more educated now to understand that. There will always be people who are biased and prejudiced. Don't yield to them. The responsibility of educating these people belongs to all of us."

We all have a responsibility to
educate against ignorance.

On September 1, 2003, a new law came into force in Ontario stipulating that when an individual exposes someone else to their bodily fluids, the medical officer of health can compel him or her to submit to a blood test. And Anderson is part of a police team that educates the helping professions about minimizing the risk of this type of injury and providing support when it occurs.

Some may think Anderson's activism has been too taxing. She admits that fighting to change the law was a gruelling full-time job, at a time when she already had two others: policing and parenting. Anderson refuses sympathy. She says her marriage, which ended a couple of months after her needle-stick injury, was already finished before her activism.

"My ex-husband is a very proud man and probably one of the most intelligent people I know. But he wasn't comfortable with me being a police officer and it caused a lot of stress. I think that incident was probably the straw that broke the camel's back for him."

As for her children, she made few compromises. She did most of her lobbying work on her days off, making sure she was always home when the kids were finished school.

It was, however, a long, hard slog. "Sometimes you feel like you're taking two steps forward and eight steps back."

But, slowly, she began to notice she had more support, and more respect at work. She received e-mails from colleagues thanking her for what she was doing. And she has the satisfaction of knowing that thanks to her, fewer people in the future will sit alone in a hospital, powerless to know whether they're facing a deadly disease.

Ironically, it was the hidden needle that helped make her into a stronger and—Anderson suspects—healthier woman. Within a couple of weeks of the needle injury, she noticed her back pain was almost completely gone. Doctors did an X-ray and confirmed the benign tumour had shrunk, and her operation was cancelled.

"We'll never know if the drugs attacked the tumour, but I am incredibly grateful it's gone. Wouldn't that be something? If this horrible incident actually led to something positive?" she says.

Anderson continues to be a widely admired police officer in Ottawa, where she is frequently held up as a role model both for the service and for women.

She stayed on as a regular "emergency response officer" until 2000, then transferred to Criminal Investigation as part of the domestic violence detective team. In 2002, she was promoted to sergeant and went to work in the Youth Section; now she is a supervisor in the Missing and Runaway Youth department. In 2003, she won the prestigious leadership award from the Ontario Women in Law Enforcement Association.

Yet, she insists she doesn't give the danger of her job a second thought. "This may sound strange, but I am not afraid of death. Because there was a time in my life when death was very much a part of my life. I firmly believe that the reason I'm alive is because I'm supposed to be. And I have a job to do and I have to do it."

DON LINDSAY

*He skipped school to protect his mother
from his father's fists and his sisters from
incest, fought his way into a motorcycle
gang, then preached his way out.*

D ON LINDSAY ADMITS he was in "a little bit of a bad
mood" the night he nearly stabbed his young son in the
hand.

It wasn't the dinner. He always liked it when they had steak
and his wife, Gwen, knows how to cook it. It was the kid, reaching across, grabbing at his father's plate, going for a piece of meat.

Lindsay felt his own knife in his hand, its serrated blade sharp.
His rage ignited and then, suddenly, he saw the knife in his big fist
poised over his son's small one. "I was on the verge of just taking
my knife and ramming it through his hand. That's sick, I know. He
didn't do anything, but that's what would happen to me."

Not just at dinner, either. Rage stalked Lindsay everywhere, revving in him the same way the engine of his Harley Davidson roared when he shredded his neighbours' lawns with his spinning tires. In his prime, he was an intentionally terrifying sight: six feet tall, 235 pounds, with long brown hair and a black leather motorcycle jacket pulled tight across granite muscles. And the eyes of a cougar. "I'd look at people and wonder what they'd do if I ripped their throat out."

Lindsay even scared himself. So, at twenty-eight, this fierce father of two sons underwent a vasectomy. "I couldn't stand the idea of bringing another kid like me into the world." He had spent most of his own childhood deflecting his father's blows and now he took what he considered the necessary step to protect any other children he might have had—sterilization.

Somehow, he had become just like the man he'd spent his whole life hating. And now, no one could hate Don Lindsay more than he hated himself.

Lindsay's father returned from the Second World War with a soldier's fists and several concussions worth of insanity. Violent, unpredictable and ruthless, he washed painkillers down with gin and vodka and vaulted from one target to the next, beating up his wife, his mother, his own children, and their pets.

Born in Toronto in the winter of 1944, Don traces his first memory to the age of three and to a sound and a sensation that would reverberate through much of his life: the human scream and its accompaniment of fear and anxiety. "I heard the screaming and the hollering from my mother. He used to hit her a lot. That is the first thing I remember."

No one was safe from his father, including the man's own elderly mother. "He smacked her right in the face. She was sitting in a big rocking chair and was knocked right over. Her glasses went one way, and she went the other."

From the start, young Don, the "other" man in the house, was on the defensive, warding off his father's attacks and trying to protect the women in his life, especially his two younger sisters. There were no holidays, no Christmas presents, no Easter; nothing but anger and abuse and unrelenting emotional erosion.

"We never had a childhood. When my father died I felt absolute relief. It was a living hell. I couldn't think of one *good* memory."

There are plenty of horrible memories, though.

Lindsay was fourteen the first time he punched his father unconscious and dragged him, by his hair, off his mother's cowering body.

He was fifteen the day he opened the door to his parents' bedroom and found his father on top of his kid sister.

And he was eighteen the first time he drove a needle full of speed into his arm.

Today, Lindsay understands that he and his sisters were the victims of severe child abuse. Back then, nobody even took the time to teach them the term. "We felt sorry for each other, but there was very little we could do to help one another in the misery. We disconnected a lot. We avoided things. We probably lived in denial, delusion."

And for eight years, they also lived in isolation. In 1947, when Lindsay was still a toddler, he and his two younger sisters were sent to a bush camp in northern Ontario. His parents, who planned to turn the place into a small lakeside cottage resort, had already shipped Lindsay's paternal grandmother up there.

The three small children and their grandmother had no plumbing and no electricity. But more importantly, the children had no real father and the grandmother no real son. Looking back, that's as close as any of them came to happiness. For the next nine years, Lindsay hauled and repaired eleven boats, cleared brush, scoured the three cottages and attended a one-room schoolhouse in the spring and fall. In winter, the heavy snow kept him away.

"Work, work, work. It was a hard life, but it was okay. We didn't have to worry every moment what our father was going to do to us. But then my dad and mom would come up and he'd blow off steam by drinking and hollering and shouting. If we didn't move fast enough or didn't get the boats corked to put out in the water, we would get hit, and my mother would get hit."

So the little boy laboured long and hard, lungs bursting and arms aching, hoping to still his father's fist. He went to sleep most nights animal-alert to the cries of his mother.

When Lindsay was twelve, his parents abandoned the property and moved all of them to a small Toronto apartment. It was a tough adjustment for three children who'd grown up in the wilderness. The familial war picked up where it had left off.

"We would call the police and when they came he would be nice to them and not let us talk to them. After they left, we'd get the shit beat right out of us. It was just hell."

Between family brawls, they moved to a small town outside Toronto. In Oakville, Lindsay went to school sporadically, bought his first motorcycle, and perfected his right hook at the local gym so he had a better chance of whipping his father in their constant fights. He mastered the art of combat in many languages: wrestling, karate, kickboxing, judo.

And the boy, who had so little, began to take what other people had.

"If I saw an opportunity to steal something and sell it, I would. No matter how big, no matter how small.

"They used to put the milk money in a little box at the side of the house. I would get there before the milkman and grab a few bucks that way. Or steal a bike and sell it. You're always thinking of ways to commit crime."

One night when Lindsay was fourteen, he was out late with his friends. His father had come home early from shift work and was drinking and badgering his daughters. By the time Lindsay returned, his mother was cowering on the living room floor; her ribs were broken and one of her eyeballs was hanging loose from its socket. His sisters were raving.

"I knew my sister would have killed him with this big butcher knife we had in the kitchen, so I had to pull her off him and pull him back into the bedroom. And he's cursing and swearing at me.

"I threw him on the bed and told him to shut up and stay there, but he wouldn't. So I go up and I punched him and knocked him out cold and just shut the door and left him in there."

As Lindsay's younger sisters approached puberty, their father took a frighteningly intimate interest in them. "He would go after them and take them into the bedroom while my mother was at work." They were just eleven and twelve, covered in welts and bruises, unable to ask for help, too ashamed to tell anyone, mute with fear. And no one, Lindsay says—no teacher, no doctor, no social worker—dared to push past his menacing father.

Lindsay became so enraged that he'd hammer the side of the house with a baseball bat until his arms were rubber. He tried to put a "hit" out on his father, but the young boxers he hired chickened out when they saw the size and ferocity of their intended victim.

The day Lindsay opened the door to his parents' bedroom, however, and saw his father assaulting his sister—confirming what he'd suspected, that his father was now raping both his young daughters—was the day *he* took control. He did it the only way his father had taught him.

"I exploded. It blew up into a whole family fistfight. Again, my mother was punched out on the floor. Him and I were fighting and smashing stuff, chairs and that.

"He would swat or slap at my sisters and they would run to the drawer and get the knives out. I just knew that this couldn't go on."

Lindsay the Protector became Lindsay the Destroyer. Once again, "I really beat him up and dragged him into the bedroom and he was finished the whole night." Then Lindsay called a friend, packed his oldest sister's belongings and moved her out. "I tried to help her get a safe place. It cost her schooling and her home, and she had to go out and get a job early," he says.

Now, he met his father's aggression head-on. "I said: 'Anything you do to Mom or my youngest sister, I'll come home and I'll do it to you.'"

He kept his word.

"He would try things like throwing a cup of tea in my mother's face or taking the supper table and throwing the food on the floor. So I started doing it to him, knowing whatever feelings I had for a father were gone. It was just a management issue."

His "skills" were recognized at his rough technical school in Oakville, where sixty students started, but only four finished grade twelve. It was the type of place where the police came into math class with their guns drawn and hauled students away, he says. When things really got out of hand, "guys busting up the bathrooms with hammers," the staff turned to Lindsay, officially dubbing him a "prefect." Unofficially, he became the school bouncer, free to fight on school property. He took great pleasure in hand-picking a gang to help him with his patrols. "We cleaned it right up. We just loved to hunt people down and give it to them."

And every guy he captured was his father. Bang, bang, bang.

In exchange for his "policing service," he says, he received an average grade of 51 percent in his courses. He was one of the four who graduated.

───────────

When you're really alone as a child, when you've beaten up your father and smashed any hope of a "normal" childhood, where do you locate "home"? Lindsay found freedom on a motorcycle, family in the local gang clubhouse. He was respected for what he knew best: violence. As early as 1959, Lindsay was the club "tester," scouting new members in bars, clubs and on the street.

"I would deliberately provoke them and see whether they shook or cried or whimpered or turned away. I wanted the guys who would come back in an aggressive way." And he was a gatekeeper—maintaining surveillance in local hotels and hangouts, always ready to fight an interloper or settle a score.

The early gangs, he says, were mainly in the business of "raising hell"—stealing, swapping bike parts, smoking pot and being tough guys.

One day Lindsay would see worse—gangs where everyone had a role: some selling drugs and running prostitution rings, some extorting money; others gambling, stealing, hijacking cars and burning down buildings. He says most of the bikers he knows were treated like animals as children, and came to behave like them as well. "They are people who are growing up in dysfunctional families and may even have a psychological disorder. They basically start with nothing."

Some day he would be able to help them, but he would have to come perilously close to losing what he loved most to get there.

Looking back on his youth, Lindsay figures the only good thing that ever happened to him was meeting a young woman named Gwen. He was seventeen and camping in Midland when he saw her with her two girlfriends. He thought she was "just a doll." She wouldn't talk to him, but he copied down her family's business phone number off the back of their pickup truck. He says he worked hard to win her over for about a year. He had to show her he was cleaning up his act before she would agree to go out with him. She got pregnant, and they were married two weeks before they both graduated from high school. He was twenty, she was nineteen. Because of the pregnancy, Gwen, who should have been going to university, took a secretarial course instead.

"I've never forgiven myself for that. She's got such tremendous potential. She could have been a special needs teacher," he says, missing the irony.

But at the time, he made a prediction that would come terribly true: "I told her when she married me that life with me would be more exciting than any other life she could have. And I kept that promise."

He says he stopped "running with the gang" when he got married, but he still kept in touch, rode and partied with the guys. He was never unemployed. After high school, he found jobs almost as dangerous as his personal life—firefighting, commercial diving, laying underwater pipes, mining, blasting and drilling.

Despite his vow to Gwen, he did sell drugs on the side to feed his own habit—speed was his drug of choice, but also marijuana, hash and alcohol.

"I was a speed freak. Oh, yeah, I just loved the stuff. It made me feel as fast as a railway train, really very powerful.

"The elation was just great because I lived in depression most of my life. It was heaven on earth just to be out of depression and I did that for years and years and years."

Shortly after their marriage, Lindsay was abusing Gwen, too, and rapidly turning into his father.

All he remembers about the first time he hit his own wife was *the rage*. "I would go off on these anger tantrums and if she was in the way, she would get hit, hurt."

It was "absolutely sickening," he says, to have become an evil, violence-lusting vampire like his father; the young Don who'd spent all those years protecting his mother and sisters had vanished.

Although he managed to hang on to his jobs, Lindsay remained a drunken, stoned criminal who hid most of his gang activities from his wife, especially the drug pushing, and crept away from his two children out of fear of harming them. "I would do a lot of bike stuff. I wouldn't let it leak home. I wouldn't talk to Gwen because if she knew and somebody came over, then she could tell. If she didn't know, you could put the heat on her but she'd have nothing to tell."

His drug habit had become all-consuming, an intricate web of intoxication spun to deaden any sensation of life.

"An average run would be: get up in the morning and take eight to ten pills. By 11 or so, I'd take another eight or ten. The pinks were 75 milligrams and the black beauties 150s—all different speed in different capsules.

"About another eight to get through till suppertime. Then I would have to start to look at getting serious to come down. I would have a drink—a bottle of wine before eight, then I'd take some Seconals, heavy-duty barbiturates for sleep, probably four or five Diazepam to calm my nerves, and top it off with five or six Nytols.

"I'd go around from house to house visiting people, anybody I knew. I'd go in their washroom and I would steal their medication. I was always doing that."

It was Evel Knievel, a well-known motorcycle stuntman, who put the waste into words. The men met one summer in the 1970s, and Knievel gave a speech comparing a drug-ravaged body to a bike engine.

"The way it looked to him is like he could buy that engine and it could have so many thousands of miles in it, but to do what he does, you punch it out, put in bigger pistons and do the heads, and you get the power. But what happens is you cut the engine life in half."

Drugs and alcohol abuse cut your engine life in half.

That's what Lindsay figures he's done. "I've cut a lot off myself and I can feel it and sense it today. I'm a diabetic. I need a new knee replacement. I've had three ankle fusions; one failed. I can hardly walk on my feet because of the sensitivity of the diabetes and it really affects my eyes. It's taken a lot of my natural strength away. So I'm feeling a great loss of energy on this end of life. I just sort of feel that I've run myself too hard and too fast."

For all the pain he's caused and the damage he's done, Lindsay is grateful he never raped or killed anyone. Not that he hadn't been willing to take out his father. He had been willing to kill himself, too—certainly, he'd been trying to do that in every fight he picked, on every motorcycle he raced, every time he took a diving job laying pipe deep underwater. One thing was certain, though: Lindsay did not want to harm his wife. But that day in 1973, as Gwen's face ground through the gravel and her shoulder slammed into the pavement, Lindsay thought he'd killed the only person who'd ever loved him.

And that's when he began to change. Some people talk about finally wising up when they hit a wall. Lindsay didn't smarten up until he slammed into a hay wagon.

The day began with a warm sun in sandy Sauble Beach, a cottage haven in Ontario. The local police had not-so-politely asked the big biker to get out of town, and were on his tail in their "bubble machines" to make sure he left. Gwen was on the back of his Harley. With one eye on the cop behind him, Lindsay kicked up to sixty miles an hour on the clear open road, heading back to Oakville.

Suddenly, a tractor-drawn hay wagon appeared in the oncoming lane and began to make a tight left-hand turn without stopping.

If Lindsay swung to the right to avoid the vehicle, he'd smash into a huge concrete culvert, but the tractor was closing in fast, so he hit the brakes.

His wife flew off the bike. Her hip smashed into the tractor's tow bar, then she cartwheeled over it and bounced down the asphalt road like a rag doll. Three of her vertebrae were compressed, her left wrist splintered and so much tissue torn from her leg that she would require knee surgery.

Lindsay slammed into the tow bar, sprained his right hand, and shattered the femur in his right leg. His right arm was partially paralyzed. Somehow, inching forward on his elbows, he managed to drag himself out of the way of the wagon wheels but was battered by bales of hay thudding down from above. Luckily, the police who'd been tailing him were there to call an ambulance.

On the way to the hospital, Gwen regained partial consciousness. She didn't blame him for the accident, but the marriage, already in serious trouble, spiralled downward, especially after Lindsay, weakened by the accident, was pushed out of his club by stronger rivals. He started spending too much time at home. "That was a real life change. When I got out of the hospital, I felt very vulnerable. I started carrying my handgun again."

For all those enemies he'd taunted over the years, Lindsay was suddenly a tantalizing target. And he wandered right into a set-up, complete with women feeding him heavy drugs in a bar until he was as soft as a jelly doughnut. He walked out into the parking lot and got "laced" by a guy wielding a two-by-four. "I was beaten half to death with my blood all over the place."

A rival gang, angry police? Lindsay had his suspicions. He never knew who beat him up that last time. But there was one thing he did know for sure: it was all over. He no longer had the power or the nerve to protect himself. Or the energy to continue deceiving his wife.

But what Gwen saw was this: that despite her near-death experience and his promises to reform, Lindsay was back to his old ways, drinking, drugging and courting violence. And he was hitting her and his children. She'd supported him through thick and thin, making allowances because of his own abusive childhood, and tutoring him as her very own "special needs" student. In her care, he'd danced through a twelve-step program for alcoholics here, a five-step program for drugs there, but he'd leave the meetings early and go get drunk. Therapists had tried to help with his anxiety and depression, but he didn't take the treatment seriously. He'd been playing a game to placate Gwen, and suddenly it became clear to her that his heart had never been in it. She'd had enough.

"It was a miracle she put up with me as long as she did. She'd recognized how screwed up I was. But she didn't want me any more and I had nowhere to go," he says.

Nor were his biker friends interested in taking care of the paranoid, limping bag of injuries he'd become. Lindsay checked into a seedy motel and puddled into despair.

Sometimes being cut loose is the best thing that can happen to you.

Gwen, on the other hand, was busy doing some work for herself after the accident. On crutches, with her arm in a cast and her sons by her side, she'd gone back to church and had made a decision to stand her ground. She'd always been tough with her husband, but he'd eluded her. She would be a fool no more.

Luckily for Lindsay, though, this woman who'd stuck by him through ugly and awful agreed to give him one last chance, but only on her—very firm—terms. He must meet with her minister, he must demonstrate real remorse, and he must transform himself.

Now, the last time Lindsay had seen a preacher come calling, the man of the cloth had finished up face down in the dirt. He'd made the mistake of dropping by to talk some sense into Lindsay's belligerent and brutal father. Lindsay's grandmother, who had called the minister for help, wound up with a beating for her trouble, too.

"My father pushed the preacher off the steps, punched him in the face, threw him over the railing, then dragged him across the grass, picked him up and threw him over the cedar hedge and fence. Then, he jumped over that himself, dragged him again and rubbed his face where the sump pump ran into the ditch."

Nothing more was heard from that preacher.

Perhaps to spite his father, then, and certainly to please his wife, Lindsay invited Gwen's preacher over. And he listened, warily at first. Looking back, Lindsay says he really had no choice: the only lifestyle alternative he was entertaining those days was suicide.

"This little Baptist minister led me to the Lord. He was just the right guy at the right time. He asked me if I believed in God and I said, 'Well, everybody does.'

"He asked me if I believed in Jesus Christ, and I said, 'Yeah, my grandmother did.'

"And he said, 'Well, how you gonna get to heaven?'

"I told him, 'Well, I didn't kill anybody, but I've done everything else.' And I gave him some excuses.

"And this little Baptist minister, he said, 'Well, that's not gonna cut it.'"

Lindsay already knew what hell felt like. He was living in it. He figured he might as well give heaven a chance. Besides, with no real home, no wife, a body that wouldn't work and no bikers to protect his back, he'd been checkmated.

The preacher stayed and talked with Lindsay, who, in turn, began to go to church faithfully. "I felt like a fish out of water, couldn't relate to the people, couldn't really understand the preaching but it made me feel like I was doing something right for the first time in my life." And it gave him somewhere to go rather than trolling the local bars or clubhouses.

It was not an immediate conversion. In the beginning he spent considerable time in church aligning his head with the parishioner in front of him so the preacher couldn't see him sleep through the sermon. Sometimes he'd chug a mickey before slipping into a pew; sometimes, he was high. Lots of times he'd just sit in church and size up the women.

One morning he awoke disgusted with himself, doubting anything could save him. He prayed that God would send him a sign if he was supposed to stick with religion.

"Then there came a rush over me as if I had done a hit of speed. It started at my feet like a wave and worked right up to my head. It was so intense, warm and comforting to the point I just didn't want to move and get up."

When he finally emerged from his bedroom, Gwen stared at him with "fear and disappointment." Quickly, he rolled up his sleeves to prove there were no fresh needle marks. "No! This is not drugs or booze. It is the baptism in the Holy Spirit."

He stayed "up" until bedtime that night, when he asked the Lord to let him sleep. And unlike a high from drugs, Lindsay says there was no "crash" afterward, no need to take more drugs to settle crazy nerves. "There was complete peace of mind."

And so Lindsay began to see life in a different way. He saw that while he was responsible for all the harm he'd caused, great harm had been done to him as well.

"Every day, the Lord watches over you. Every day you can do better by him and that makes you matter."

Don Lindsay became a Christian on January 7, 1974. It was the first club he'd joined that didn't want him to hurt anyone. And Lindsay figured that if someone as esteemed as Christ could forgive him, maybe he could forgive himself, too.

"I had to take on my own ego and my pride and my identity. They were all defence mechanisms to keep me strong, to protect me from all the fears I had growing up."

Once he hated himself less, he had less drive to hurt himself and others. And once he stopped hurting people, he began to see how much damage he'd already done. His first acts of love and pleas for forgiveness he made to his wife.

"I would tell her I loved her. And I really loved her. Many times I was thinking of taking a step backwards again, but I knew it would be a mess because I finally realized, 'This marriage goes along real well as long as I do what you tell me to do.'

"It hit me right after that: these are what I call little divine inspirational things. You know, since I've done what my wife has said,

I haven't been to jail. I haven't had to pay restitution. I haven't had to go to court.

"And really, it's not so bad. I'm thinking: What a profound revelation? But what a dumb dummy I was."

Around the same time, Lindsay joined an outpatient rehabilitation program at the Addiction Research Centre in Toronto and kicked his speed habit, along with a handful of other street and prescription drugs. He received psychotherapy and psychiatric treatment and was prescribed anti-anxiety and anti-psychotic medication. It turned out that he had been using speed to mitigate the effects of his mental disorders for all those years. Once he got the proper medication, it helped him kick his addiction. It would take him much longer to get his drinking under control.

To hate yourself less, stop doing hateful things.

Slowly, a strange, sad-eyed butterfly was wriggling from its straitjacket of addiction and self-hatred. An astonishing symbol of change, a grey-haired biker clutching a Bible instead of a gun, Lindsay began roaring around on his motorcycle trying to help stop fights rather than start them.

Increasingly, he found himself being asked to intervene informally—to help break a family out of the gang lifestyle, to counsel a man who was selling drugs or abusing his wife, to spring someone from the crime cycle. Just as he'd been asked to use his brawn at high school to solve problems, he was now being asked to use his Bible.

Once, a speeding car screeched to a halt in front of him and a half dozen bikers pulled him in. He was scared. "Turned out, though, they didn't want to beat me up, they just wanted to confess and find out whether they were going to hell."

Lindsay was also pondering the huge disconnect he saw between the people who needed God's help—bikers, crooks, addicts—and the churches that were trying to provide it. "The churches didn't make sense to them, didn't speak to the problems they were having. I know when I was in those regular churches, the minister must've had a drink three hundred years ago, and he can't relate to me in any way."

And the thirst in Lindsay to help was growing stronger every day. He wanted to offer a hand to the people he'd left behind. He joined a motorcycle club for Christian men and had trouble keeping quiet. "I had to focus on giving my testimony and actually resist the urge to preach. Things that were working for me, small victories that I had experienced and the peace that I knew, were worth sharing with others. It's hard to keep your mouth shut when you have found the way and have some answers."

Lindsay enrolled in a small Bible training centre in Hamilton. He took courses part-time for two years, certain with every passing moment that he'd finally found his "calling." He was ordained in the Evangelical Church Alliance in 1980. He moved around, providing pastoral counselling to bikers, gang members and anyone who had difficulty being understood or getting help.

In 1994, he brought his special brand of populist, all-accepting evangelism to the Grace Bible Fellowship Church in Wasaga Beach, a popular biker hangout in Ontario. He is a full-time pastor, who also helps run the busy food bank and charitable thrift store. His anger management and crisis intervention programs are teeming with referrals from the police, doctors, lawyers and court officials.

There are only a few rules in his church, but they are strict ones: honesty, freedom from judgment, and a determination to be the best possible person.

Judge no one. Criticize no one. Gossip about no one.

And while it did not occur to him when he first took up preaching, Lindsay now thinks he's atoning for some of the damage he did. "Much has been forgiven, and much is required. I am paying my dues back to society in a positive way. But I'm also feeling that I am doing what I was created and given talent to do."

Much is forgiven, but much is required.

After his father died in 1973, his mother married "a wonderful man" who made sure the rest of her life was filled with love and adventure. His sisters have also married "really good" people. His two boys are now men themselves, and despite residual anger about their father's past, "we're a very tight family." He marvels sometimes how so many really fine people managed to find their way into the shattered lives of the Lindsay family.

As for the perpetrator of Don's terror, he's been forgiven, too. "I believe that my father hated himself for his own behaviour. He was enslaved to his own addictions, violence and pattern of abuse and was also filled with guilt, hatred and shame."

Lindsay believes that forgiving his father not only released him from constant emotional turmoil, it "releases forgiveness to me for my sins."

Pastor Lindsay now spends a great deal of time in jail, ministering to murderers and thieves and abusers. "I don't get caught up in what they do. Just as Christ doesn't. They are still people. He loves them, but he doesn't like their sin. It's sort of like me. I like the person but when they do their lying and conning and two-stepping, that's where people get hurt."

Lindsay is very connected these days, not just to dope smugglers and delinquents, but to counsellors and psychiatrists and drug recovery programs. He's on the other side of the fence now and he's reminded every day how much he regrets his past.

"I do so much drug and alcohol counselling, working with criminals, and I have a real distaste now for somebody bragging about something evil they've done, because I'm always working with the victims, and that ticks me off. Or people getting kids stuck on cocaine and then I end up having to clean up the mess."

For all his tragedies, though, Lindsay isn't bitter about what he's endured. He sees it as a special education, part of his life's ultimate work.

Some lessons you can only learn in life's classroom.

"I know what I've learned you couldn't get in university or in Bible school. I primarily deal with broken people in all different forms. But I have lived all those forms, too."

He feels equally grateful for the lessons garnered from his physical pain—the diabetes and damage wrought by years of drug abuse; arthritis from his bone-splintering motorcycle accidents; the memory loss and emotional scars from constant beatings.

"If you are suffering, I understand how you're feeling. I know what it's like to have operations and broken bones and more operations. It's almost like a whole language that I've been able to learn to deal with people."

The language of suffering is universal.

Ironically—or synchronistically—he spends much of his time rescuing people from the motorcycle-gang lifestyle that once gave him refuge. And a lot of time getting women out of the clutches of violence. He uses a technique he learned in prison called "tough talk."

A churchgoer who insists on dealing cocaine on the side is going to face Lindsay's wrath. He's gone from pitchman to preacher: "I can stop you, or I can turn you over to the police and they can stop you. Because you aren't winning and if you're doing this you don't care about your family. The things you say and do should line up with love. If the things you do line up with and cause hurt and pain you're not a lover, you're a hypocrite, a con artist, a liar.

"And that's what I face. That's the language I gotta use."

Lindsay masterminds "interventions," too—rescue efforts where he helps pluck kids from abusive parents, battered wives from psychological traps, families from their own homes after they've been invaded by motorcycle gang members.

"A lot of times, I'm not only a minister, I'm a social worker. Sometimes I have to speak to women who are being wiped out through the abuse of their husband," he says.

"That criminal thinking, what he's doing—and he's using all the excuses in the book—but criminal thinking is a need for power and control, resentment toward authority. And I have to say, 'This is the way your husband really is. This is why you're having problems. Because he doesn't think of you as his sweetheart. He only thinks of himself. And he uses some excuse to try to fly it by you and you're being the nice little wife; you buy it and you get hurt, more and more and more. And then you start to come apart.'"

Lindsay teaches family members that they must set rules and regulations for abusers: "Don't tell me you love me and then turn around and smack me in the face. Don't say you love your family and then spend all your paycheque on dope. There's no excuse for that. None."

Pulling families from the clutches of motorcycle gangs is also extremely dangerous. "I get a phone call and some guy wants to get out of the club and maybe some of the club guys are actually living in his house now. So the husband and wife want out and they own the house. But they're watched a lot."

A covert operation, sometimes months in the making, is set in motion. First, the couple consolidate their cash, begin to shut down accounts and then, one day, the husband quietly moves the wife and children to another province or country. Just before the man leaves, he hires a couple of lawyers who will concentrate on evicting the gang members and then selling the house.

Sometimes Lindsay must go even further to rescue people, to do for others what was never done for him as a child. For more than twenty years now, he and Gwen, who is also a pastor, have opened their home to some of the most troubled children in Canada, including very tough young offenders. They're both certified as "specialized treatment" foster parents for "emotionally and behaviorally disordered young people." They've had more than forty such kids in their home: every one of them is a chance for Lindsay to lift the needle on a skipping record. He is giving young people what he needed himself. "Life has been very much a full circle."

There's no question that Don Lindsay—still a huge man with masses of greying, wiry hair braided down his back, meaty fingers laced with heavy silver rings, and wary eyes—is a force. But his injuries and ill health put him out of the tough guy's game a long time ago. He admits it takes far more strength and courage to stay on his path of love.

"As long as I stay out of a mental institution and as long as I can walk the streets sane and sober, I'm making it for me. I know people who come back and they aren't doing so hot. And there are those who never made it. So I see myself as a success in that realm of beating the drugs and coming through the hell that we come through."

SHEHEREZADE ALAM

Sheherezade Alam's husband and eldest daughter were murdered in their home— by a guest who brought a pistol to tea.

FROM THE START, the weekend was momentous. An enormous storm had covered Toronto in a thick white mattress of snow that undulated over roofs and porches and across broad lawns all the way into the groves of High Park, where only the tips of tall statues peeked out.

Sheherezade Alam, with skin the colour of toasted almonds and deep brown eyes, was wrapped as always in layers of handwoven fabric, ruby and pomegranate, tangerine and turmeric gold. She had never seen so much snow. With her long hair of black and silver tucked inside her winter coat, she pulled on her snow boots—an exotic costume for this woman born in the heat of Pakistan on the other side of the world. She opened the door to the pirouetting snowflakes and laughed.

Thinking back to that day, Alam, a potter, says, "I'm just on such a high, living life and being out in the open, I walk and walk. I know until my new pots are glazed I shall not sleep, but I have had all this fullness of the day."

She plunked into the snow, bottom first, then fell back onto the cold bed, fanning her arms and legs to carve an angel in the snow beneath her. Because she is an artist she saw not only her imprint but the untouched snow around it, the trees laden, the sky a blue-periwinkle-silver, the stormy backdrop of a Canadian snowfall. She breathed in the immensity of the cold, the energy of the storm, then returned, empowered, to her art studio that Sunday afternoon. For hours, she bent over her whirling potter's wheel, spinning new and brilliant pots to life and icing them with glaze. Too excited to sleep, she works far into the night.

Is it shock that forever sets in memory those moments just before tragedy? Or is there a grand pause, a massive shudder in time and fate, as the apocalypse approaches?

There are few clues in the day-to-day events, the details of time before tragedy. Often there is happiness.

Alam's husband, the internationally acclaimed painter Zahoor ul Akhlaq, had recently completed a retrospective in Karachi, Pakistan, and was spending some time in the family home in Lahore. The couple's elder daughter, Jahanara, at twenty-four a talented dancer, had gone with her fiancé to join Zahoor there. In about a month, Alam and their other daughter were to join them for a holiday, just as soon as the nineteen-year-old Nurjahan had completed her final high school semester in Toronto.

On this snowy Sunday night, Alam is exhilarated by the rush of inspiration and near-completion of "key" pots, which she believes mark growth in her artistic style. Finally, she leaves her studio and slips back into her apartment, where she sleeps peacefully until nine o'clock the next morning. She awakens hungry for breakfast. She begins preparing a fruit salad. Looking back at those moments years later, she will vividly recall each fruit segment, sheathed and glistening. The milky membrane of the orange, the thin red arc of skin on the crisp apple shards, the phone ringing.

The phone ringing.

Hello?

A friend from New York. A friend from New York is on the line. He wants to know whether she has heard the news and, in the ensuing silence, realizes that she has not.

He cries out.

"Oh, but how can I tell you? How can I tell you *this?*"

Sheherezade Alam is almost as old as her native country, born the year after a British lawyer drew a line across the top of India. Her parents settled in Lahore, near the eastern border of the fledgling Pakistan created by political fiat in 1947, and plotted their daughter's new life. Like them, she and her two brothers would be well educated, although as the only girl in the family she would be expected to marry and settle near her parents.

Her father, an executive for a cement company, had money and access to power. Her mother, an innovative educator, established the city's first kindergarten and used art—music, dance, play—as teaching tools. So, unlike most of the young girls in her community, Alam was encouraged to explore her artistic abilities; she was given lessons in everything—ballet, piano, accordion, fine art, horseback riding. The family home was filled with handmade art, Sheherezade's summers with exotic travel. Always, there was the emphasis on education and intellectual exploration.

Perhaps her parents should have been less surprised, then, when Alam defied class and gender to devote herself to clay. While studying at the National College of Art, she decided that she wanted to do what other women in Pakistan did not: she wanted to get as close to the essence of creation as possible. As waves of industrialization replaced hands with machines, she felt a need to preserve the traditions of her country. "I was very aware that we were going through a crisis in craft, and I wanted to continue in some way this huge heritage. The value of the handmade object was of great concern to me."

Socially, her profession was considered shocking—"because there are no female potters," Alam explains. "Women are decorators. They're helpers, traditionally, but they're never the pot makers. I mean that my hands were covered with clay all day. Really!"

Male artisans who came to visit were "horrified" to see Alam, the striking and accomplished daughter of "such a good family," coated in clay, her legs spread wide around her potter's wheel.

"But I found it very invigorating. It touched me, so that I felt very good about what I was doing." And Alam knew herself well: years later, clay—and the lessons of its eternal life cycle—from earth to art object to dust again—would save her life.

Alam heard about Zahoor ul Akhlaq before she met him. Already immersed in his postgraduate scholarship work at London's Royal College of Art, her future husband was seven years older than she, and at twenty-seven already a popular intellectual and painter. They met through mutual friends while she was in London, where he enthralled her in the galleries and museums. When he returned to Pakistan the following year, he immediately swept the young art student into his cultivated circle, introducing her to creative minds and new ideas about Marxism and feminism.

She and her friends would visit him in the apartments once occupied by Rudyard Kipling, where they would dine with artists from around the world. She was in awe—though not intimidated. "He had this rather soft, absent-minded demeanour, but was very interested in what I was doing or thinking. I found it very exciting intellectually, me finding my place."

Akhlaq encouraged Alam to do whatever she pleased, to break out of the confines of convention and weave a life as bohemian as her love of pottery. But her mother and father were apoplectic, and—like so many worried parents throughout history—ordered an immediate separation of the two, who though aware of a growing attraction were not yet lovers. Foolishly, her parents banished her to Paris. Alam was delighted. "Paris! Can you imagine? I was sent off to the most romantic city in the world to change my mind about love!"

In what Alam also sees as a stroke of karma, she was paired up in France with another respectable daughter—only to discover that like her, this young Frenchwoman was struggling with a secret love, also a man who didn't have her family's approval. Together, the besotted women vowed to follow their hearts, not their families' wishes. More than thirty years later they remain the dearest of friends. They married their true loves within a day of each other and never regretted it.

Alam accepted Akhlaq's proposal and flew back to Pakistan without telling anyone. On her wedding day in 1971, she did not paint her hands with henna. There was no sari of gold and red. And no parents either. Instead, she donned her blue jeans, braided her cascading hair and exchanged simple vows with the famous artist on a beach in Karachi. The moon was full and the scent of flowers embraced the small gathering of friends.

But the next day she awoke with knots in her stomach as she imagined breaking the news to her family.

Months would pass before Alam's parents agreed to meet the husband of their only daughter. They did, however, send a car every weekend to convey their daughter home to the family compound; her husband was not invited. Alam agreed to the arrangement, believing she was striking a compromise between what she needed and what they wanted.

But any lingering strain between Alam and her parents evaporated when her first daughter was born. The light-footed, always-waltzing Jahanara, whose arrival melted the pride of all. She was, from the start, a magical being, Alam says. The small family moved into Alam's parents' large household with its many comforts.

The couple had their second daughter, Nurjahan, in 1979, but Akhlaq's eccentricity and growing fame were placing demands on Alam. "He had no sense of time. He would roll in at four or five in the morning without calling. He had a huge inner landscape with which he was connected, and thought out things deeply, so he would almost disappear into himself."

Clingy and weepy at first, Alam eventually realized her husband's independence was an invitation for her to establish her own space; that freedom would produce in her an inner strength. "I knew I needed to create my own track," she says. She never suspected, however, how much she would need this power later.

With her husband's support—and her parents' promise to look after her young children—Alam spent a year studying pottery in England, then returned, invigorated, to her clay studio under the mango trees. Later, she would accompany her husband as the international community beckoned him: Best Art Teacher award in Pakistan; exhibitions in London, Paris, Tokyo, and Venice; a rare Fullbright Fellowship at Yale Institute of Sacred Music; teaching in Turkey; and an invitation to work in Canada.

And it was in Canada, on that white Monday morning in 1999, that Alam's glorious life shattered.

As her friend stammered on the telephone, she pressed him. His wife had been ill for a long time and she suspected the worst.

He could barely breathe the words.

"Have you heard?"

"What?"

"Oh, how can I tell?"

"But you must."

"Zahoor has been killed."

"Oh. . . ."

"And also Jahanara."

"Oh, oh . . . And how?"

"Shot. Murdered. I cannot go on. I will call you later with more."

Orange segments in their tissue-cocoons fall to the carpet, the juice weeping into the ancient wool. A door closes somewhere in the apartment building. The phone, instrument of pain, sits silent.

———————

Later, she collected the details of death. But she would never be able to make sense of them. It turned out she knew the young man who murdered her husband and precious daughter. He was a serpent, who had come as a guest to her beautiful home in Lahore —the Garden of Paradise, they called it—a friend of two drummers who frequently came to play for the popular and talented Jahanara. Alam had made him dinner, invited him to sit with her family. He had sipped her soup and listened to the esoteric conversation that flowed from the creative minds of her family. He had smiled and shaken hands with the painter he would later kill at point-blank range. This made her nightmare more excruciating.

She now had to live with the knowledge that the murderer had lingered in the home she shared with Akhlaq, a sanctuary filled with souvenirs of love, of trips taken together, markets searched, ideas transformed. The home of Sheherezade and Zahoor was a work of art. Besides his massive oil canvases and her sensual pots, there were carpets and sculptures, bronze and copper, silk, tapestries and antiques. Artists from around the world had gathered at their table, debated their callings, created together. "There was the huge devastation of how it could have happened in that very home, which had seen such extraordinary moments."

Why he murdered her family does not matter. Perhaps it was his growing devotion to Akhlaq, or a crush on Jahanara gone wrong. Perhaps the bullets were to ensure they would not leave and return to Canada without him. Perhaps, she says, he was simply crazed by drug use and the frenzied chaos that is often the mood in Pakistan.

It does not help Alam to know that the assassin had been invited in for tea that morning but had declined, saying he would return later. That he did come back while Akhlaq was discussing books with a colleague, and Jahanara was down below getting the house in order for the next day's Eid festivities; Jahanara's fiancé, Alnoor, was sitting by the fireplace, studying.

The assassin walked straight up to Alnoor and shot him in the temple. The bullet snapped through his head and his jaw, yet he managed to stagger to Jahanara's room, desperate to warn her. The killer took another path through the house, hunting Akhlaq, and murdering him as he sat with a friend. He shot the friend, as well. Then he fled down the front stairs of the house only to see the lovely and terrified Jahanara. He looked down at her, raised his gun and shot her through the head.

Alnoor, breathless behind him, collapsed in a passing rickshaw and was taken to hospital.

Four people shot, her husband and daughter dead.

"Senseless things happen that we really cannot understand. I do not really go into it any more. I take it from the point that it happened and that I have to grow and evolve from that fact," she says.

We all experience shock differently. It filters through the terrain of our childhoods, over the rocks and moss of our inner landscape, which is blooming or barren depending on what came before. Alam's reaction was creative and transcendental: her awareness expanded rapidly; her sense of the universe exploded along with her heart. She felt old and wise, large and omnipotent—all at the same time.

In Toronto, the moment after receiving the ghastly news, she looked out the window at the sky, at the world that only moments before she'd beheld with wonder. Later, she would be unable to identify the source of her initial calm, that sense of extreme, all-knowing wisdom. That courage was imbedded in her terrain.

And so she was able to say, "Okay. The incomprehensible has happened. I really felt that it had happened. There is no way, I thought, that this could not be possible. You can go on afterward saying, 'This couldn't have happened,' but not at that moment. It was accepted."

The wiser, older soul continued to speak to her, through her.

"At that moment, I understood that life is a gift and it is given and it can be taken away. It was a very core belief within myself, that everything that I've been given is a gift, and I have celebrated life as a gift."

And slowly she was saturated with her daughter's spirit, and with the knowledge that rather than small and dead, her child was bigger than ever.

"She's everywhere. She's in the stars. She's in the moon, she's in the flowers, she's been released and delivered back to the universe. They had now become part of one another."

She is in the stars. She is in the moon.

Alam had been reared as a Muslim and accepted early that "there are mysteries we'll never understand." She felt the wisdom coming from the universe, she says, from something earthy and unknown.

Still, it was not only Alam's tragedy; she moved slowly down the hall. She must tell her youngest daughter. She had no idea what to say. How do you deliver such a devastating message? Yet, she felt strangely confident that words would come if she opened her heart.

She sat on the bed. She touched her daughter's shoulder, all warm with sleep. She waited fully ten minutes as the nineteen-year-old slowly resurfaced and focused on her mother's sad face.

"Nurjahan, I have something very important to tell you that will change our lives forever."

Her daughter's chin shot up, her eyes scared. "Is it Baba? Is it my father?"

"And Jahanara, too," Alam said.

Mother held daughter for an eternity, rocking her as they wept. At ten o'clock, Alam's friend came over for coffee, as she did every morning. Charlotte, hearing the news, immediately started to rally all the friends in their artists' co-op to help. The phone began to rattle again; relatives, friends who had heard. Alam's brother was already on his way to Toronto from New York, hoping to cushion their grief in person. He was there by noon.

Then, suddenly there were plans to think about, plane tickets to be reserved. Funeral arrangements. Family to be notified. And what of their apartment? In the midst of cosmic chaos they grasped at domestic order. But already they were different. Husband gone, one is less wife. Sister gone, the other is less baby sister; father gone, she is less child.

"I was amazed at what Nurjahan said, how she walked with me," Alam recalls. "It wasn't as much mother and child, but as friends who were now facing this squarely in our own lives."

The younger woman offered the older woman two pieces of advice.

One: "We are going to walk through this one baby step at a time," Nurjahan said. When they felt overwhelmed, they would stop. When they were ready, they would inch back out again into the world, and move just a tiny toe-length forward.

Two: "We must remember to love ourselves, too," she added. Because there are moments during the experience of tragedy—

and over great, vast expanses of time, as well—when one feels utterly lost, alone, surreal; when suicide becomes a possibility, if only fleetingly, because you want to "disintegrate, disappear."

But loving oneself makes killing oneself out of pain far more difficult. When we lose a loved one, for a time it is as if we have lost all love. We have been hurt, trashed, tortured, battered. We need to be held, comforted, soothed. Often the one who would do this best is the one who is no longer with us. We must take up where they left off, love ourselves as they have taught us to do. When we are hurt, we must take better care of ourselves than ever.

Yes, Alam whispered, love ourselves.

And then the inevitable practical matters of death arose—the funeral, the clothes and belongings that must be touched, folded; the beloved lingering scents inhaled, wept over.

For Alam, there was another unspeakably dreadful practicality—the trial of the man who murdered her daughter and husband. She chose not to attend and still, today, refuses to talk of vengeance or retribution. "I can cry a lot, but it is not about being angry. It's about being sad. Anger takes me nowhere."

Her family in Pakistan handled all the legal details, the serpentine path to conviction in 2002. The assailant's motives remain elusive. She has no desire to search for them. There was a time when she imagined meeting the man and asking him how he could do such a thing, why he would.

"Yet I knew it really was not going to change a thing. I won't get the answers. Even if the assailant gave me answers, there are no real answers as to why this could happen, and that's why I do not have the questions, either."

Do not live in the "what if" days before the tragedy.

Asking why is simply the wrong question, she says, because your true goal—somehow explaining the inexplicable—can never reverse the outcome. "I accepted what I could not change."

And while some of us heal better if we confront our attackers, this is not Alam's way. "He is not somebody that I give that importance to. I feel that I should raise the dust somewhere else. That is more interesting and more meaningful."

And yet despair came for her, too. Despite her courage and her determination to continue, she bobbed and swayed and risked, more than once, sinking into the deep lagoon of depression. "Oh, what is the point?" she would think immediately upon waking, feeling fine for a few moments before sleep's cruel trick of dreamy peace receded. "What is the point of living without all of them?"

Nor could she stop searching for her lost ones—actually looking up when she heard a footfall, jumping up to greet them as a door opened. "In life they were so large, so physical, so very present. How could they just disappear? I saw the burial, so I knew that the physical had been buried. But spirits so big cannot evaporate, I thought."

She was haunted, until she felt she could endure it no more. Despite her daughter's earlier entreaties, suicide beckoned. She threatened it repeatedly. Finally, a friend called her bluff. "You're right, Sheherezade, you cannot see any reason to go on. So, jump off the building. Jump."

It was a risk only a knowing friend could take. And it worked. Invited to do the worst, Alam saw clearly a choice between life and death—and she balked. Of course, she realized: ending yet another life made little sense. It was the endings that caused the pain. "Oh, no! I can't. I've only been pretending. I do not have the courage to kill myself. I do not want to die. It is not my time. There is more I have to do. Having lost love, I *knew* how immense love is. And it is because I *knew* love that I had to continue."

And she'd had an epiphany, which suddenly came back to her, crystallized. Several weeks after the burial in Lahore, she'd been walking slowly along a worn path that joined her parents' house to her own, looking at the sky and thinking how life, really, was over now. She'd seen the best of everything. It had been up, up and magical. Extraordinary things had happened, exciting journeys, and now it was going to be the opposite.

It was at that moment that Alam heard the voice, at once her own and yet from another place, asking her, "How can you doubt something that's happened so often in your life? Something incredible has happened before and it will continue to happen, and I have to find out where."

Life, she realized, is a precious celebration, not a guarantee, but a daily gift. Her gift would continue.

Life is a celebration, not a guarantee.

So she took her pain back to the pottery wheel and allowed clay to comfort her, again. And there, watching the wet lumps ooze and bend and slowly take shape, she saw the entire cycle of life and the inevitability of death in every life. Death, she realized, is hard to endure because we do not accept its inevitability; we do not see it as part of the practice of life. But as she worked in clay, that lesson, that evolution, was constantly unfolding before her, forcing her to understand, to give up the same "clinginess" she'd first felt for her husband.

"Clay is life. It's identical to what happens to you. You start, begin, you grow, you form. Pots have the same body parts as human beings. There's a foot and a belly, a shoulder and a neck and a lip."

But moulding clay, like living life, is very difficult. You have to be tenacious. "It has some very difficult moments but you have to persevere. So clay teaches you about attentiveness, about honesty, truth."

The more she gave herself to her clay, the more she healed. "You're just clay, too. You're malleable. You have reflections of that as you work: what the clay is making you do. It's a kind of a dance—the making, the drying, and the firing. Running around after each part, chasing the clay, and taking it on a journey, like raising children. You want it to look a certain way. It's very transformational and it transforms you, so you grow with each stage, each part."

To rail against death, when it is so inevitable, is futile. Clay will harden, clay will crack, and clay will once again become dust. She understood most deeply now the advice of her old mentor. Shortly after the murders, when she asked him what to do now that so much was lost, he had said simply, "Continue." And she had another insight: she must continue if the past was to have any meaning.

"If you think everything has stopped, create something. Start the process, a new process, all over again. You are here still and therefore have the opportunity—are meant to take the opportunity by accepting grace, which is a gift from the universe—to continue and evolve."

If you think everything has stopped, create something.

Alam, although she refused to ask questions about her past, had firm answers for the future. Would she allow a deranged stranger to physically kill her husband and daughter and then spiritually take her life and that of her remaining child, as well?

No!

Would she let the assassin extinguish Zahoor's and Jahanara's achievements, destroying the artistry and legacy of her beloved painter husband and dancer daughter?

No!

Or would she use her grief—the power of tears and loss—to give strength to their voices? Rather than burying those she loved, Alam decided she must raise them up.

"It was about how I processed what this was all for. Is it so someone can kill huge potential and beauty, or do you bring more energy to that potential—and share it?" Her loved ones had built lives of creation, community and the extraordinary.

With the "loving support of amazing friends who supported, encouraged and held me at every step—like angels," Alam began to create again. First, she arranged for Toronto photographer Richard Seck's magnificent photographs of her husband's paintings to be reproduced on thick, silken paper in a small book, titled simply *Zahoor al Ukhlaq* and published in 2000. In a sparse, moving text written for posterity, architectural scholar Roger Connah writes that the murders were events of "such incomprehensibility, such senselessness, that it would leave a family, a community, and whole parts of two cities, Lahore and Karachi, totally bewildered. That such persons could no longer be allowed to live caused a paralysis."

Alam says the book kept her going through 2000.

Soon after, Alam launched another and even more ambitious project to honour her husband. She asked artists from all over the world to send her paintings on *takhti*, small writing tablets made from *partal* wood, which grows in the foothills of the Himalayas. Her husband had been fond of using the wooden tablets as a painting surface. She received more than eighty takhti— from Indonesia, the United States, Europe, Canada, Morocco— and put them on display with Akhlaq's work. Alam hopes the extraordinary show, which premiered in Canada in 2003, will circle the globe for years, to remind us of the obligation we all have to "continue," and to illustrate the healing benefits of doing so. "The show talks of a journey through love and creativity, which is obviously very similar to the journey of life."

For her lost daughter Jahanara, she archived videotape and photographs of her dances and her poetry, creating a documentary celebration of her art and continues to share the images on film and television with artists' groups and students.

And she has begun to dance, although she never did before. "Perhaps only children will ever get to see," she laughs. Each morning, she turns on the music and spins and weaves, and knows that it is the soul of her Jahanara moving her feet and bending her at the waist.

"My husband and my daughter will always be with me. There will never be a time when there is not desperate sadness, when there is not *missing*. It is as it should be. What I must learn, though, is to process it. To confront the grief directly and say, 'I know what happened. I can endure this. I will carry it with me in a way that makes me stronger.' I will carry their love by continuing to love beauty."

> ***There will never be a time when there is***
> ***not sadness—that is as it should be.***

Death, like life, is a part of the human journey; rather than hide it or see it as the end, Alam says she is struggling to weave its presence into her life now. To feel belonging, we must know loss. Happiness, sadness. To know harmony, we must fight and survive. To know love, we always risk one day losing it.

And as Alam honours the lives of her husband and her daughter, she is more determined than ever to seek her own path, until her own pot cracks and begins the inevitable journey back to dust and then to clay and to pot again.

"Do you think that I will ever lose my great mentor, who taught me everything? I think clay has actually brought me through this trial, like a teacher, like a mother. Like some source of energy that was given to me and taught me and watched me grow."

As an artist, a woman, a creator, Alam says there are no longer any barriers to her imagination. When grief broke her heart, it also washed away her limitations.

"The impossible happened. But if that which we can never imagine can happen, anything is possible. Anything beautiful, too. So, now I can dream impossible dreams."

If the impossible can happen,
then anything is possible.

She has decided to remain in Canada. Pakistan is still too full of memories. It is a place, she says, where she grew her "old skin"—the skin that knew the touch of her loved ones and lost it. Now, she says, she is growing her new skin; a skin, she hopes, that is more resilient, more enduring, less a shroud of mourning. But she will never forget.

The morning of September 11, 2001, Alam turned on the television and ached for the people killed in the terrorist attack on New York, as well as those left behind to yearn for them. And she was reminded, again, that all of life is evanescent—no matter how vast our collections, how great our stockpiles, how tall and strong our buildings.

"I think again of change. Of how we have to always be ready for what is to come. Life is always change, but it was so dramatic on September 11, so fast. In such a short time, I know it creates an even stronger impact."

Remember that life **is** *change.*

And when lives are taken in violence and in hatred it makes the acceptance of death even more challenging.

"Processing hate, pain and death is transformational, because it takes you to that point, to the incomprehensible. It pushes you to another reality."

To survive the saturating sadness, Alam says we must first feel and face it. And, then, "Make something out of it. Make something real all over again, starting from the beginning."

To overcome the emotional paralysis of loss, we must see it not as an end, she says, but as a call to action in our own lives. It is the next step in life, not the last one.

"It's how you evolve through something that is so devastating, how you arise from the ashes."

And in speaking of grief, she is not shy. It is, she's discovered, a universal language. Her dialect is one of hope: "I tell every single person I talk to about grief that it will change."

"You're going to be a very happy person again. I tell them that Jahanara and Zahoor are just on the other side. I feel like there is a kind of veil between them and me. I can't see them, I can't touch them, but really their presence is there."

KENT LAIDLAW

Through the despair of rape, murder and tragedy, a seasoned police officer battles clinical depression—only to uncover his deepest humanity.

WHEN CALAMITY OR TRAGEDY comes knocking, many of us discover that we have hidden resources we can summon to help us cope: a sense of self given us by loving parents, optimism born of happier times, perhaps a special friend or teacher whose confidence in us became our own.

And some of us do not.

Some of us never knew those nurturing supports. Some of us never got what we needed to build our adult backbone. Yet even without those reserves, from the barest beginnings, we can create our own ability to survive, and eventually give comfort ourselves.

It is often those who've known loss or sadness who are best able to help relieve it in others.

Kent Laidlaw, tough, muscled and keen-eyed, spent more than three decades as a top cop; but what he saw in the last year of his career shocked him as nothing before ever had, and made him rethink his entire life.

Laidlaw grew up beside a small forest in Aldershot, Ontario, with mainly wild animals for friends. He did have parents like most people, but they were not like most people's parents.

His father rushed home from work around five, stripped off his customs officer uniform, grabbed something to eat, hit the sack for an hour, jumped up, brushed his teeth, pulled on his tuxedo, rushed out the door to the local (or not so local) dance hall and belted out songs for the rest of the night. "So that's the way it was," Laidlaw says.

He saw his mother a little more, but her full-time job in sales management kept her tied up, too. "They weren't home much."

He taught himself how to ride a bike, teetering and crashing until he dared push off from his tiptoes and test his balance, with never a steadying hand on his back.

He taught himself how to play baseball, throwing the ball high in the air and racing round to hit it, pitcher and batter in a single boy. He doesn't complain, though. That's just the way it was.

"I didn't have anyone there. I thought that's what everyone did. It wasn't until I got much older that I realized that this was a role parents, fathers particularly, might have played. My dad just wasn't there. He didn't have time."

In part, Laidlaw figures his parents were working hard because they needed the money. His father, a government employee who'd signed up with the Air Force during the Second World War, was late coming home because of a serious wound. He arrived back in Canada in 1946 after an extra year convalescing in a British hospital, and eventually bought a house for the family with the help of a veteran's loan in the then-tiny town of Aldershot. It soon became a struggle to pay all the bills.

Laidlaw suspects there was more to it, though. And he often wonders whether his parents had even wanted children when he was born in the last month of 1939, just before his father shipped out. To soften his memories, he imagines what it must have been like for his young father after war and wounds.

"Imagine: he comes home late and he's got this very attractive wife and I think he wants to party and have a good time. He's been in England all this time in the hospital and here's this five-year-old son who he doesn't know, hasn't spent any time with. I think that was a bit of a shock for him. But I'm surmising. I really don't know."

What Laidlaw did know was what it felt like to be alone, although he insists that he was rarely lonely. "I had the animals. Our house backed onto a large park of crown land. I'd spend hours in there all by myself checking out the animals, listening to what's going on."

With no one to help him with homework and few kids his own age in the neighbourhood, Kent Laidlaw quickly fell behind in school. He played football, joined the army and air cadets, but felt like an utter failure every time he opened a textbook. And though he would go on to be a highly promoted and well-respected police officer, praised for the skill with which he handled some of the country's most grisly rapes and murders, he can still remember the first really painful moment of his life, the day he stuffed his feelings inside and bolted the door.

Grade five. Math class. He didn't know the answer to the question on the board and he knew his teacher *knew* he didn't know the answer. But she didn't care; she'd been riding him for a while. Now she made him stand up beside his desk for everyone to see. There was a big steel heating grate in the floor and little Kent stared into it, praying he'd fall through into the basement.

He would have given anything, he says, not to have to stand there, humiliated in front of his peers. "That one class probably set me back about twenty or thirty years, because when I left I was absolutely convinced I was stupid and it stuck with me for a long time."

It would take years and someone else's mistake to restore Laidlaw's confidence. In the meantime, the only places he felt vaguely valuable—and part of a family—were on the football field and in the cadet corps. He spent hours playing high school ball and later coaching; he rode the bus every week to air cadet training.

His parents were disappointed when he dropped out of school, but somewhat assuaged when he got work as a labourer in Hamilton's steel mill, laying hydro lines and doing office work. They put their foot down when he eyed the Navy, but were pleased when he talked about policing. It seemed a natural fit for a guy like Laidlaw, who was athletic, aggressive and knew how to play by the rules. And the Burlington force, later the Halton Regional Police, was willing to take him in 1961, with only his grade ten education. Despite his dismal luck in high school, he consistently scored high on policing exams, first at the Hamilton Police Academy, and later during advanced training at the Ontario Police College and Canadian Police College.

As a newly minted beat cop, he admits he felt "absolute fear" the first day on the job. "I nearly wore the shoulder out of my shirt because I was rubbing against the windows and buildings to keep as far away from the road as I could in case someone stopped and asked me a question."

The first person he arrested was a former high-school classmate, whom he found drunk and folded over a fence. He hauled him up on his shoulder and deposited him in jail—gently. "When you know the right thing to do is put your old classmate in jail to protect him from hurting himself, you know you were meant to be a police officer," he says.

Laidlaw rose rapidly through the ranks of the force—beat cop, sergeant, inspector, superintendent, and executive officer to the chief of police.

And then one day, his over-committed boss asked him to stand in for him at a luncheon speech. The chief had a few notes, but there was no time to prepare, so Laidlaw stood for the first time behind a podium and gave a lecture on police management, off the cuff. As so often happens when we speak about what we know, Laidlaw was competent and compelling.

Afterward, a university professor in the audience congratulated him on the quality of his presentation and wanted to know where he'd earned his postgraduate degree. "I thought, okay, you know, now's the time. Do I tell the truth and tell him that I dropped out of high school after grade ten or do I just play the game?"

Kent Laidlaw told the truth. "I said to him, 'Well, I've never been to university, and I didn't even get through high school.' I can't tell you how good that felt for me to be able to say that."

The professor, however, blanched. "You could tell that he regretted terribly having been so complimentary because I wasn't part of academia. So that was very, very enlightening and very empowering," Laidlaw says.

It was proof that even without a formal education the police officer had more than his share of life lessons to impart. "It was a major breakthrough for me."

Couple his emerging confidence with his taste for overwork and you have a formula, albeit not a very healthy one, for a stellar career. Laidlaw rapidly became one of the province's staunchest and stealthiest narcotics investigators. In the 1970s, the wealthy town of Burlington was overrun with drugs. Laidlaw and his partner at the time took the problem very seriously.

"It was really bad for the size of the city and for the population. Both of us took that on as a personal agenda. This simply wasn't going to be allowed. We had an informal arrangement that we would work all night. We would lie on the grass behind a drug trafficker's place or whatever it took. And our informal agreement was that we wouldn't book any overtime unless we made an arrest."

By Laidlaw's calculation there is a police chief out there who owes him "something like two thousand hours of overtime that he was always promising to let me take as Friday afternoons off to go golfing. Well, I don't golf and the Friday afternoons never happened."

Although Laidlaw married and helped raise two daughters he loves dearly, he admits he worked too hard. At one point he and his wife, from whom he is now separated, also opened a bakery. They both worked an average of eighty to ninety hours a week. Besides being a full-time police officer, Laidlaw was running a business, coping with sales, taxes and demanding deadlines. "Our conversations got pretty terse and short at times, and our patience with the kids was less than it should have been."

Years later, Laidlaw says he still loves his wife and is incredibly grateful to her for putting up with "some crazy times."

They eventually sold the bakery but Laidlaw kept the pressure on himself at police headquarters. He made his name as a good manager, developing protocols and strategies to help officers on the more traumatic calls, one of which was notifying families of death. His curriculum vitae had become daunting: uniformed patrol, youth bureau, drug squad, criminal investigations bureau, criminal intelligence unit, duty inspector's unit, courts and community relations bureau, command of the criminal intelligence bureau, chair of Criminal Intelligence Services Ontario, founder of the Halton Regional Police Service Victims Services Unit.

The higher his rank, however, the more out of touch he felt with the cops on the street. Finally he decided that it was something he needed to fix if he hoped to have a shot at the deputy chief's job. So at his request, Superintendent Laidlaw was appointed district commander for the City of Burlington in 1991, just weeks before what would come to be hauntingly known as that city's Summer of Sorrows. Laidlaw's plan was to get back into the operations side, the part of the job that made him feel most alive.

But he would receive more hands-on experience, endure more trauma, counsel more victims and see more fear in those hot, sad months than in his entire thirty-year-career. And it would spell the end of policing for him. "That was the worst year of my life."

There was no advance warning. He looked forward to his first day on the job. He would be supervising some 125 staff members in the busiest police division in Halton Region, and it was exhilarating to again be able to walk to work in a friendly town, where the officers swung out onto their shifts with cheery goodbyes and returned in a flurry of slamming locker doors and whistled hellos. He was respected. He was competent. He was in charge. He loved it.

And then it began.

One soft June evening, six high school students packed themselves into a friend's car and set out to "fly" across the rolling highways of northern Burlington. If you pushed your speedometer high enough and hit the right rise on "Roller Coaster Road," your car would "sail" in open air for hundreds of feet. Police and parents hated it, but their warnings weren't enough to deter thrillseekers from "catching air" on Number 1 Side Road. This time, the sixteen-year-old driver was too inexperienced—having received his licence that very afternoon—and couldn't regain control of the car as it flew over the crest, slapped the tarmac and waffled violently into the ditch, landing on its side in a twisted mass, sealing the kids inside. The fuel line ruptured, the hot gas drizzled onto the engine and flames licked the car. Panicky neighbours emptied fire extinguishers but couldn't prevent the blaze from reigniting each time it ebbed. By the time ambulance, fire and tow trucks arrived on the scene, the car was a ball of fire.

Four teens in the back seat could not get out and no one could get in. Through the flames and heat and acrid smoke helpless bystanders heard the wail of dying children. Some of the young passengers hadn't even known the boy who drove them to their death. "The officers were traumatized," Laidlaw says. "It was such a useless, senseless waste of life."

Two tow-truck operators lost their nerve for the job that afternoon, and needed counselling. Devastated firefighters and police officers tried to cope, some of them by hiding their feelings, others by quietly seeking out professional help. Laidlaw remembers how moved he was by the anguish of one of his crew, a tough 240-pound officer, reduced to nerves and shakes.

"The officers were really, really distraught because they stood there and all their training and all of their skills and everything they had was of no value. And these youngsters literally died within three feet of them."

The little town was not accustomed to tragedy. But just three days after the crash, another teenager, fourteen-year-old Leslie Mahaffy, disappeared from her Burlington neighbourhood. She'd known some of the Roller Coaster Road accident victims and had been seen at their candlelight vigil.

At first, police treated the case as a missing person file, because Mahaffy had a history of breaking curfew and leaving home for short periods, Laidlaw says. And unbeknownst to the public, police were also getting some bad information: Mahaffy's friends, thinking they were protecting her, were lying, telling police they'd seen her recently.

"So we thought that she was alive and probably staying with some friends, and it wasn't an issue. But in fact she was probably dead by the time that happened. That was very, very difficult for us."

When human body parts encased in cement were discovered two weeks later in Gibson Lake on the outskirts of Burlington, many officers were certain they'd found Leslie Mahaffy. Forensic specialists disagreed, however; officers were dispatched to reassure the Mahaffy family that the dismembered body was not Leslie's. "When we all knew in our hearts that it was," Laidlaw says.

A few days after the Mahaffys' fears had been calmed, forensics called to say they'd changed their mind. The decapitated and dismembered body was Leslie Mahaffy's, after all.

"But those people who made the initial decision to say it wasn't Leslie weren't the people who had to go to the door and say 'You know what? There was a mistake made here. A terrible, terrible mistake and, in fact, that is Leslie. That is Leslie.'"

But how did District Commander Kent Laidlaw end up in a motel room in northern Ontario delivering that horrifying news when it wasn't his to deliver?

On the day police received the new forensic report confirming Mahaffy's identity, there was a knock at Laidlaw's door. One of the detectives assigned to tell the anxious family had come to ask Laidlaw to excuse him from the duty. He had a daughter Leslie Mahaffy's age, he said, and he admitted that he just couldn't face it.

"It was really interesting because the 'old' me, the traditional cop, would have said, 'Listen, I don't wanna hear about it.' Fortunately, I had grown and matured to the point that I was proud of him. I told him I'd talk to his boss and that I was proud that he had the courage to come to me. That's not easy."

Finding a replacement wasn't easy, either, until someone turned the tables on District Commander Laidlaw. "Hey, Super, don't you *teach* this?"

There was a pause. Laidlaw had developed a respected method for "death notification," and he'd earned a reputation for victim support. He was the expert, but he had not volunteered to go. Looking back, he says he was in denial.

The silence continued until Laidlaw made a decision that would change his life.

"You're absolutely right. It is the place for me and I should be there. The community deserves that a senior officer be there." He apologized to the junior officer for not being quicker off the mark.

But the fact was, admits Laidlaw, "I didn't wanna go. He didn't wanna go. None of us wanted to go." What he didn't say was that he too had daughters at home, one of them the same age as Leslie Mahaffy.

At night, Laidlaw had gone home and knelt by the beds of his sleeping daughters, guilty and weeping, yet deeply relieved. "Why are they alive, why are they spared? How can we be so lucky?"

There were 122 paces to the front door of the second-floor motel room where the Mahaffys were waiting, and avoiding the media. Laidlaw counted every one.

In his head he reviewed his protocol. He'd taught hundreds of police and emergency workers how to break the painful news of a death in the family: normalize it. Deliver the information effectively and clearly so that they can understand. Try to keep emotion out of it. Communicate simply. This is the most important message that a human being will ever deliver to another human being. He'd taught it a dozen times.

Yet when Laidlaw knocked on the door and it opened, nothing came out of the veteran officer's mouth. Laidlaw and his colleague stood silently. The Mahaffys stood silently. "The moment they saw us they knew. I remember feeling so totally, totally useless. For all of our training, and all of our good intentions, everything that we bring to this is of no value because it was too late. And they knew."

The district commander sat down beside Dan Mahaffy, Leslie's father, and asked himself, What can I say? There are no words. Help me, please. What do I say?

Tears began to stream down Dan Mahaffy's face as he sat on that worn settee in the little rented room. Laidlaw wrapped his arm around the man and they cried. Not a word had been exchanged.

That was probably the night Kent Laidlaw began to fall apart. Tiny, hairline cracks in his psyche, likely there for a long time, began to split and fan out silently across his self-confidence, undermining all that the strong, seasoned police officer had become. Did he feel the whispered approach of depression and ignore it? Perhaps he didn't have time to think about it. Suddenly, another Burlington teen was missing.

Nina de Villiers went jogging near the city's prestigious Cedar Springs Racquet Club in early August and vanished. One minute she was running, head up, lungs pumping with fresh air; the next, there wasn't a trace of her.

Laidlaw was responsible for mounting the largest ground search to date in Canada, complete with cadaver dogs, helicopters and 3,500 searchers. Hundreds of civilians desperate to help find Nina were turned away. And everywhere there was panic.

"I think one of the failings of the police community sometimes is that we don't admit that we're as frightened and as desperate as we are, and we're struggling the same as everyone else. I guess you can't do that and maintain public confidence, but often that is the reality for us."

One week later, the worst possible outcome: Nina de Villiers was discovered face down in a creek near Kingston, shot in the head. Within days of finding her, police linked her death to a suspect, who had just been tracked to a shopping mall while being pursued for another crime. Cornered, Nina's killer shot himself in the head.

The seasons pressed on, oblivious to the town's anguish. A burnished autumn, a pale winter and then, as spring flowers bloomed and kids peeled off their heavy coats, another young girl, a fifteen-year-old in a private school uniform, vanished, leaving behind nothing but a shoe.

Kristen French had been missing two long weeks when Laidlaw was called to a crime scene in north Burlington. A knot of stunned officers stood above a ditch, looking down. There, resting now in some awful slumber, was the tortured, raped and strangled body of the missing girl.

French had been kidnapped and murdered in St. Catharines, then dumped on Number 1 Side Road, where the four teens had died months before.

Laidlaw asked a few quiet questions. He was grim but calm. Inside, he was reeling.

Who was doing this?

How do you stop an invisible maniac?

What could he do?

What could he do?

Was anyone safe on Kent Laidlaw's watch?

For months, frightened parents had been calling, begging to know whether it was too risky to send their children to school. One woman met him on the lawn of the police station in the early morning dew, demanding to know whether it was safe to even allow her daughter outside. It ate him alive that he didn't know the answer.

After thousands of police hours and old-fashioned slogging on the part of many, many officers culled from around the country, the Scarborough rapist, Paul Bernardo, and his wife, Karla Homolka, were caught. They would eventually be imprisoned for the murders of Leslie Mahaffy and Kristen French.

The kidnapping and killing stopped, but nothing would ever be the same. "It was said at the time that Burlington lost its innocence and that was so very true," Laidlaw says. "It was just so overwhelming that those tragedies happened and in such a very short time frame."

And for Kent Laidlaw it was tragic timing, too. Because when the senior officer first arrived in Burlington at the beginning of the Summer of Sorrows, he had a secret. By the end, that secret was too big to keep.

Less than a year before he transferred to Burlington, District Commander Laidlaw was standing behind his desk at division headquarters. He was leaning against his chair trying hard—too hard—to make up his mind. The veteran cop just couldn't decide whether he should sit down or stay standing. Sit down? Stay standing?

Move the chair and sit in it. Or just stand. Sit or stand? Stand or sit? Sit or stand? Stand, sit, stand, sit? Stand, stand, stand? Sit?

"That decision was beyond my ability to make at that point. You talk about gun calls and risks and violence but nothing was as frightening to me as that moment, because I am a Type A personality, a control freak, a perfectionist, all those sorts of compulsive behaviours. And then suddenly I cannot make a simple decision. I couldn't decide whether I should sit down. I knew something very, very serious was going on."

He'd helped develop the police force's employee assistance program, so Laidlaw knew who to call when a cop needed help. But the psychologist was floored to see the senior officer himself arrive for the appointment. It took a moment, but the therapist regained his composure and inquired about Laidlaw's symptoms. He put out his hand and asked to see Laidlaw's datebook, then flicked through half a dozen pages. He shook his head and placed Laidlaw's tiny black book beside his own big datebook.

"I run a busy practice," the therapist said. "I book people every fifty or fifty-five minutes, but my schedule pales in comparison to yours. Who is doing this to you?"

Laidlaw thought. "I am."

The psychologist diagnosed a major clinical depression and advised Laidlaw to check into the hospital that afternoon, or begin taking antidepressants. "Those are the two options and one of them has to happen this afternoon," he said.

Laidlaw felt trapped. "My first reaction was to say, 'Screw you, I'm not doing this. I am out of here.'"

But the evidence against Laidlaw was too convincing even for him to ignore: he couldn't make decisions; he was barraging himself with work. Night after night he told his wife he wanted to lie down for a quick nap after dinner, only to fall into a dead sleep until it was time for work the next morning. He was numb. He was exhausted. He was lost.

So he filled the therapist's prescription and took the drugs. "If I could have handled it, I would have already handled it. I couldn't."

If you can handle a problem on your own, you probably already have.

In today's world, where a stigma still lingers around psychiatric illness, it is difficult enough for any employee to admit to depression. But how could the top cop, the professional who was supposed to keep the community safe, admit he'd had a breakdown? Laidlaw was determined not to be perceived as weary or weak or mentally ill—especially not *mentally* ill. "It was not an environment in which you were encouraged to come forward."

Within several months of that first session with the therapist, however, Laidlaw wound up in the psychiatric ward, dreading the sound of the hospital doors clanging shut—leaving him, a high-ranking police officer, on the wrong side of a lockdown. It took him a while to grasp the irony: the stress "expert" who had encouraged his subordinates to speak openly about the emotional strain of the job had spent months, if not years, in total denial of his own eroding emotional health.

From the beginning of his career Laidlaw had simply filed away his painful memories. Under the letter "D" was stuffed the death of the infant he'd tried to save after the baby's head got stuck in the bars of a playpen and no one called an ambulance; the blame laid on him by the hysterical mother; the cold, blunt words of the nurse who told him to go home because the baby was dead. Not a word of comfort because he was a cop.

Under the letter "L" for loss he'd hidden the death of his own stillborn baby daughter, whom his wife had carried to term. He'd filed it away immediately so that he'd be strong enough to call all of the relatives and channel the sympathy to his wife.

Under "S" he'd stored the shock of being told his father was dead and the memory of being led by hospital personnel—too coolly and quickly—to his father's body after they saw his police uniform. Under "M" for murder he'd put the tragic death of a female friend at his own cottage. She had been beaten to death by her boyfriend, and, for a brief time, Laidlaw himself was a homicide suspect.

Yet although Laidlaw noticed he was shutting down, speaking less and sleeping more, he did not or would not see this as a symptom of anything more than overwork.

How typical, Laidlaw says, that he was the one who preached openness, the one who assured officers it was a sign of courage, not fragility, to expose their emotional underbelly. Yet he'd let himself down. "Yeah, I believed it, but I didn't believe it for me."

When you're handing out advice, start with yourself.

And that denial, he came to realize, was one of the "flaws"—as he puts it—in his make-up. But denial is also a symptom and a working component of depression. Emotional suppression and stress had pushed him into a dark zone. Hospitalization, medication, therapy, deep introspection and his faith in God brought him back into the light.

He stopped shaking long enough to discover his real emotional age: a little boy of nine who'd been humiliated in math class and left alone far too much. He came to realize he'd gone through his entire life protecting the sensibilities of that kid, with police training, promotions and discipline. "He got stunted somewhere along the way and never matured. I was able to overpower the fear most of the time, but it got to the point I couldn't do it any more."

So, falling flat on his face was the best thing that ever happened to District Commander Kent Laidlaw.

If you are flat on your face, consider it
may be the best lesson of your life.

For the first time, he acknowledged the fact that he hadn't turned to anyone for emotional support because he'd been raised with no one to turn to.

From therapists he heard the words "abandoned as a child" and unwillingly rolled them around on his tongue. It took time—and talking—but he learned how to weigh more accurately the burdens he'd been carrying. He let down his guard, a little. For twenty-eight days, he watched the world go by from his hospital window and saw that it continued without him.

And so it was that fresh from therapy, with depression seemingly lifted, Laidlaw found himself in Burlington, ready to take charge.

Were there clues he was cracking under the pressure? Or that the mind of the man, smart enough to protect itself, was temporarily shutting down? The most obvious was the job itself: high-stress work done against a backdrop of moral depravity, and in a maelstrom of human grief and unanswerable expectation.

From early in the morning, sometimes up at five right through until he fell asleep, exhausted, on the living-room couch, Laidlaw was moving at a frantic pace: briefings, officers' reports, phone calls, meetings, media interviews, strategy sessions, along with all the other police calls, which didn't go away even though Burlington was tracking a psychopath; and perhaps most trying for Laidlaw, the constant barrage of insistent questions from civilians and the media.

"One of the most stressful aspects was the huge amount of media attention and their expectations of accurate information. Much of which we did not have at that time. The entire community was looking to us for answers—answers we didn't have.

"And all of us had the normal family and personal commitments that were present after work. These circumstances applied to all of the officers involved, not just me. My officers made huge sacrifices in terms of their personal lives during this period."

As the grisly spate of crime drew to a close, Laidlaw again felt that unwelcome visitor: the sucking darkness of depression, the pit of quicksand he'd been scrambling to avoid since his release from hospital. One day, as he sat quietly looking out the window, he felt its heavy presence—oh, so bleak!—like a curtain descending, suffocating him with despair. "That's when I knew it was happening again and I absolutely had to do something about it. That this was all too much," he says.

Kent Laidlaw is no longer a police officer. After his recovery, he discovered he didn't have the stomach for policy wrangling and internal politicking at the police station.

"But the more significant reason I think was that I now knew how vulnerable I was to the stresses and I honestly felt that if I stayed it would destroy me. I felt a bit like a boxer who'd reached a point where he needed to quit at the top of his game, or leave punch drunk. I survived as long as I did in no small part due to some of the outstanding and dedicated peers and subordinates who worked with me."

But Laidlaw wasn't prepared to take an ocean cruise just yet. He wanted to help victims—to evolve from the man who caught their assailants to the man who stayed behind afterward to help restore some faith in life.

"When this all started, I'd have given anything to have had someone come up to me and put their hand out and say, 'I have some sense of where you're at and can we talk? Could we have a coffee? Could we spend some time together?' The offer was never made. And as employers, friends as human beings, we owe that to one another. We're always so afraid of offending. That's an area where I thought I could help."

> *It is through helping others that*
> *we often best heal ourselves.*

He joined the steering committee for the sexual assault and domestic violence suite at Joseph Brant Memorial Hospital, and worked for the Ontario Attorney-General in victim services. And since he'd developed the first Halton Police employee assistance program and also been instrumental in the victims services unit, devoting time to people doing that kind of work was a natural next step. "I found a corner where there is so much more work to be done and I wanted to be there for people."

He enrolled in every specialized course he could find, making it all the way to Washington, D.C., to train with the National Organization for Victim Assistance, eventually becoming a member of their international response team.

And that's how a former Burlington police officer wound up in Bosnia. Laidlaw admits his initial zeal to help others may have led him to get in too deep and go too far afield for his emotional balance. When he arrived in Bosnia in 1996 as part of a NOVA humanitarian mission, it was only a couple of weeks after the civil war ended.

The mission was undertaken to help counsel survivors in Srebrenica and Tuzla. For two weeks, Laidlaw stumbled through villages that had been burned to the ground, where women and children told of watching their husbands and sons and brothers massacred in front of them, of women, young and old, who'd be repeatedly beaten and gang-raped.

"I was confronted with a whole society that had so many layers of grief that I'd never encountered," Laidlaw says. He felt overwhelmed again, unable to offer much in the face of vicious hatreds and violence, on a scale beyond anything he'd seen as a cop. Frustration and helplessness began to stalk him again, but this time he was not alone. None of the volunteers felt able to stay inside that inferno very long.

Just before the team was set to leave the war-ravaged town of Tuzla, some thirty women gathered in a school that was being used as a refugee centre. Through his translator, Laidlaw asked whether the volunteer teams had managed to help in any way. The crowd parted as an elderly woman made her way from the back of the room. She sat beside him, weeping quietly as he spoke.

Then, through the translator, she responded: "I don't know much about you. I don't know what your education is or your training, but my answer to you would be that you're the only people in the whole world who cared enough to show up."

And so it was that Laidlaw learned from a Bosnian grandmother that he mattered, that everyone mattered. "And that at any given time you can be the only person in the world who's there, who shows up, and that's worth more than money, more than all of the university degrees and the procedures and the policies."

At that moment, Laidlaw also realized what needed fixing about his own perspective: the scale was wrong. He saw a huge problem, imagined he had to solve the whole thing—all the fear and death in Burlington, all the anguish in Bosnia—and felt totally at sea. Now he came to accept that a single moment, a single person, a solitary gesture, can make a difference. The only gesture too small is no gesture at all.

No help is too little.

Kent Laidlaw cherishes different memories now.

He remembers, for instance, that feisty little woman in her eighties who refused to be turned away from the search for Nina de Villiers. The woman who insisted she be allowed to speak with the officer in charge, then opened the trunk of her car. Inside, Laidlaw saw a huge cake with thick icing. She'd baked it that morning. She didn't want to join the search, after all. She understood that hundreds more people than could possibly help had shown up: she just wanted to feed them. "They're going to be hungry," she said, and gave him the cake.

He remembers the long, grim shape of Rocco de Villiers, Nina's father, who according to strict police policy was kept at a distance from the frenzied search for his daughter. Laidlaw broke the rules, inviting him into the police command post, hoping that he'd feel more empowered if he could see how hard everyone was working to find his little girl.

He remembers his intense fear when Leslie Mahaffy's mother was asked publicly to appraise the job he and his colleagues had done in notifying her family about her murdered daughter. "I never felt we could do enough. I was so afraid she would be critical. I felt we'd failed. But she said she saw how hard we tried. It was one of the biggest reliefs of my life."

Laidlaw left the police force but he remained an officer. He'd seen how computers could assist in the search for criminals, so he brought that methodology to tracking and helping victims. In 1995, he launched his own Web site called "Canukcare," an Internet clearinghouse for advice, advocacy, training and resource materials. Today, he works as one of the most sought-after "trauma responders" and mental health advocates on the continent. He's trained as a hostage negotiator, crisis responder and is one of the few Canadians certified by the American National Organization for Victims Assistance.

But he's no longer hiding behind his uniform; he's out in the field telling the truth about isolation and depression.

He's telling his story so others will understand it is essential they tell theirs.

He's putting out his hand and offering a cup of coffee to anyone who looks as if they need to talk.

Dr. Graeme
Cunningham

Mary
Brown

Mulugeta
Abai

Doug
Dane

Rose
Handy

Vince
Savoia

Jaene
Castrillon

Pascal
Ribreau

Isobel
Anderson

Don
Lindsay

Sheherezade
Alam

Kent
Laidlaw

Acknowledgements

I am grateful and deeply touched by the people who have inspired and supported *A Quiet Courage*.

The "Courage People," who helped me tell their stories here, who read these pages and showed bravery and conviction at every step in the hope that their experiences will help others.

Isabel Bassett and Nancy Chapelle of TVOntario and Beth Haddon, who have always supported *Person 2 Person with Paula Todd*. And TVOntario for generous permission to draw on our television interviews. Series producer Liane Kotler and Karen Pinker, my program co-creator, who bring creativity and commitment.

Hard-working and talented producers Leora Eisen, Susan Ferrier MacKay, Kate George, Eric Geringas, Robert Prowse, Cristina Senjug and Litsa Sourtzis, who proposed these remarkable people for interviews and who, along with supportive TVOntario crew, editors and managers, including Wally Teska, Christine McGlade, Ken Hillier, Kevin Glecoff, Mario Resnik, Maurice Dalzot, Doug Beavan, David Cheung, Tom Ford, Paul Boisvert, Tom Savage, Dean Henry, Marisa Gatto, Paul Colbourne, Horst Mueller, Brad Bakelmun, Paul Spencer, Marc Porter, Julian

Lannaman, Ted Ambrose and the late Herb Langwasser, brought their stories to life on the program.

Friends and colleagues for insights during the writing: Sally Armstrong, Jane Jankovic, John Honderich, Susan Swan, Janice Stein, Richard Gwyn, Eliza Mitchell, Diane Rowe, Nan Mantle, Rosemary Hnatiuk and Valerie Miller, our compassionate friend who seems to have always been with us. More who helped: Alice Lopers, Dalma Szabo, Annie Gelfand, Donna Wood, Rosemary Brdar, Yvan Richards and Doris Fusco. And my co-host at TVO's *Studio 2*, Steve Paikin, a good buddy both on and off camera.

My stepdaughters, Jennifer and Robin Grant, whose generous love makes a world of difference. My father, Jim Todd, for his care and constant repairs; my mother, Joyce Todd, who showed me the joy of writing from the beginning; my sister, Janet Fahmi, an early and encouraging reader. Tyler Fahmi, the genius behind www.aquietcourage.com.

Team Weekend for unwavering friendship: Gary Forshaw, Allyson Forshaw, Laurie Monsebraaten, Jeff Keay, Jeffrey Long and a special thank you to Silvia Presenza for her advice, discipline and fabulous food.

There would be no book and no one to thank were it not for the good people at Thomas Allen Publishers: president Jim Allen, whose integrity pervades the firm (thanks for the title!); publicity manager Alyssa Stuart and managing editor Jim Gifford for their expertise. As for the professional recognition editor and publisher Patrick Crean receives, I can report that it is utterly deserved. It was his scouting that found me and his encouragement, editing and creative guidance that put this book in your hands.

Finally, I must thank three people without whom I cannot imagine the outcome. If books are like babies, Frances Petruccelli has been an extraordinary midwife. I will be forever grateful for her research and editing skills, her tremendous organization and boundless energy. Ralph Fine's enormous talents, fine intellect and exuberant friendship saved the day more than once.

And, finally, my wonderful husband, Doug, who read, edited and endlessly discussed the manuscript, and generously made room for the Courage People in our life.